Wanderlust

Wanderlust

Compiled by:
Laura Fokkena
Heidi Sandler

iUniverse, Inc.
New York Lincoln Shanghai

Wanderlust

iUniverse, Inc.

For information address:
iUniverse, Inc.
2021 Pine Lake Road, Suite 100
Lincoln, NE 68512
www.iuniverse.com

ISBN: 0-595-32683-8

For our grandmothers:
Hilda Fokkena, Jeannette Henke, and Gerta Pfeifer
and in loving memory of Gertje Lüken, Johanne Fecht,
and Gesine Harms

Contents

Acknowledgments

Vielen Dank:

Gerda Taylor, for translating, fact-checking, and nagging us to get this book done;

Clara Hinman, for researching, providing memorabilia, and keeping a million names and dates in her head;

Wilfried Penning, for translating, explaining obscure German references, and putting up with being discussed behind his back;

Jens Pfeifer, for translating, putting words to song, and having trans-Atlantic online discussions;

Lenore Palmer, for hosting guests, playing tour guide, and for being an excellent storyteller;

Connor Durflinger, for creating our cover art, assisting with graphic quality control, and helping us avoid technical meltdown;

Manfred Becker (http://www.ostfriesen-info.de/), for the use of selected photographs;

...and everyone else who answered our many pleas for information.

~Heidi Sandler

Preface

This book began as the story of three sisters and their descendents. Johanne, Hilda, and Jeannette Lüken, the daughters of Habbe and Gertje Lüken, grew up in a village in northern Germany in the first half of the 20th century. In the 1950s my grandmother, Hilda, left Germany with her husband and three children and moved to America. A few years later she was followed by Heidi's mother Gerda, the daughter of Johanne ("Hanni"). Gerda's mother and brother Garrelt stayed behind, as did Jeannette ("Netti") and her family. Hilda's daughter Meta moved back to Germany, but her son Habbo—my father—stayed in America. Growing up I remember thinking of Heidi and her brother Phil as "my American cousins" and everybody else, including those on my grandfather's side with whom we had less contact, as "my German cousins." Today Habbe and Gertje Lüken, or "Opa Walle" and "Oma Walle" as we still refer to them, have six grandchildren, eleven great-grandchildren, and seven great-great-grandchildren.

Yet as Heidi and I began collecting these stories we realized that it was impossible to limit our definition of "family" to those who were directly descended from Oma and Opa Walle. Others brought a unique perspective to the story we were trying to tell, as can be seen from the letters my mother, Clara Hinman, wrote to her parents during her first trip to Germany in 1968. Because my uncle Willie was killed in a car accident two years before I was born, I was particularly pleased that a high school friend of his, Mike Heffner, offered to write about his memories of him. I'd grown up hearing many stories about Willie as told by older family members, but this was my first time reading the perceptions of someone his own age who knew him well. Likewise my own tribute to Richard "Tink" Palmer—technically my father's sister's husband's sister's husband, or "uncle, of sorts"—seemed an appropriate fit, despite the distant link, because Tink had always been such a presence in our lives.

Heidi and I also realized that we couldn't limit ourselves to the German-American experience as we had originally intended. Ostfriesland, the region of Germany where the Lüken sisters lived, is geographically small and contains a relatively homogenous population; the pieces we received depicting this area will be recognizable to anyone who has lived or traveled there. Writing about "America," however, proved more complicated. Like many second- and third-generation immigrants to America, Oma and Opa Walle's many grandchildren have blended backgrounds: they are part African, European, Arab, and South American, Jewish and Christian and Muslim; they have lived in Utah, California, downtown Boston and Washington, D.C., the mountains of Colorado, a sleepy Arizona town just north of the Mexican border, Alaska, Minneapolis, in suburban Chicago, and in rural Iowa. Writing about America necessarily means embracing varied perspectives. To that end we chose to include Ray Brost's memories of Wisconsin in the 1940s, Gunda Brost's comparison of the America she visited as a child to the America where she is now raising her African-American son, Connor Durflinger's thoughts on Boston and the American Revolution, and the funny, frenzied travelogue Lisa Fokkena kept while driving throughout the country, by herself, at the age of twenty-three. German heritage factors into some of these accounts in significant ways and in others not at all, but all of them convey a sense of *place*, and together we believe they tell an interesting story of what it means to be an American.

The last limitation we dropped was that of form. In the beginning we had imagined that the book would be filled with memoirs like Gerda Taylor's description of her childhood in Germany during World War II, or Habbo Fokkena's account of immigrating to America in the 1950s. In the end, however, we were unable to leave out Phil Sandler's fictional story about a son and his aging father, since we felt it communicated more about that particular relationship than a straightforward essay ever could. Nor could we pass up the chance to include the various tidbits we received as we were pulling this volume together, including letters, song lyrics, eulogies, photographs, a parable, and contributions from our children. Finally, this book would not be complete without including some of Willie Fokkena's poetry.

Due to the limitations of our publisher we were not able to include works in languages other than English, so the contributions we received in German have been translated. We have set up a companion web site to this book at http://www.heidisandler.com/heimat/which includes the original German versions of these pieces, as well as German translations of a few of the English pieces. The web site also contains links to information about Ostfriesland—the region of Germany where many of these stories originate—as well as maps, photographs, and sound clips.

~Laura Fokkena

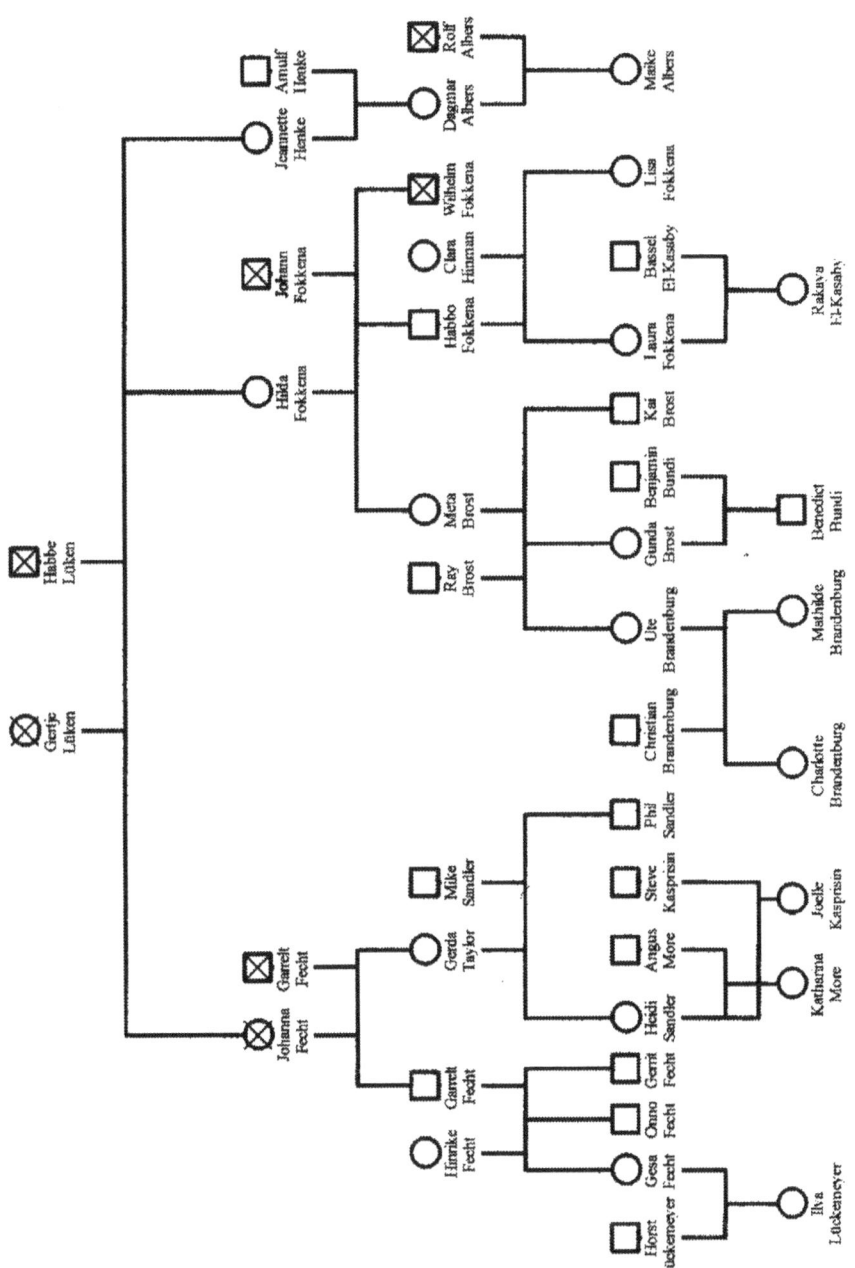

Die Heimat ist in den Herzen die sie lieben.

(Your homeland lies in the hearts of those who loved you.)

~Epitaph, tombstone of Johann Fokkena (1911–1993)

Heimweh, Fernweh

By Laura Fokkena

My images of Germany always involved inverted dunce caps. I blame my aunt and uncle for this. Every year they sent us black-and-white photos of another miscellaneous cousin wearing white tights and a dirndl dress (or—worse—black socks and lederhosen) posed smartly in front of a nondescript brick building carrying a *Zuckertüte*: a large cardboard cone, nearly the size of the child himself, filled with candy. "German children," I was told, "receive this on their very first day of school."

It was a tradition. Germany was filled with traditions. Unlike America, where I was unfortunate enough to have been born, a country with no traditions at all, flat, Heritage Lite.

The *Zuckertüte* was not the only advantage of being born in Germany.

"German children holiday in Italy."

"German children drink wine at the dinner table."

"German children begin learning English in fifth grade. Then they take French, and Latin, too. By the time they get their *Abitur* they are fluent in seventeen languages."

Such tales spill from my grandmother, my Oma. She is a thin, suspiciously active woman, her long gray hair pulled back in a sturdy bun and covered securely with a hairnet. She wears house dresses and sensible shoes, an apron, horn-rimmed glasses, and speaks a halting blend of German and English that she adopted when she first arrived in the United States, a sort of Germglish which has neither improved nor worsened in the last forty years. Her loyalties to Germany and the United States are as divided as her linguistic abilities: she resists this land of Burger Kings and Lean Cuisine, of Kmart and Kool-Aid and watered down beer and, God forbid, Wonderbread, yet she still gets tears in her eyes when I plunk out "America the Beautiful" on her untuned piano.

"The good America," she calls it. "*Tja!* Thank God we made it to the good America."

Oma's house is a creaking monstrosity set dead on Main Street. This is Clarksville, Iowa, population 1,400: one of those Midwestern hamlets still filled with farmhouses, giant old buildings with hardwood floors and unstable porches, each construction altogether unlike the one next to it, yet the lot of them looking sufficiently congruous when you survey the town as a whole. The houses are bigger than your average split-level ranch-style home with wall-to-wall carpeting and fake fireplace, and more aesthetically pleasing, too. Oma's house is even larger than most, with four big bedrooms, three walk-in closets, a wraparound porch and a mammoth basement complete with what should be a wine cellar but where she instead stores four million potatoes for the upcoming famine which, she insists, could be right around the corner. It's why that half-eaten sandwich is stuffed in the back of the refrigerator, too. ("It's a Depression holdover," my mother explains. My American grandfather stockpiles food, too.)

This is the kind of house that should be filled up with children but is instead filled up with furniture. For while no one can accuse Oma of squirreling away useless bric-a-brac and silly mementos, she is not one to boot a perfectly good bed to the curbside just because no one has slept on it in thirty-five years. Therefore every room in the house is furnished, despite the fact that only three of them—the kitchen, the bedroom, and the living room—are used on a daily or even weekly basis.

When I stay overnight, however, it's different. During these times I get to sleep in the featherbed with Oma while Opa, my grandfather, gets evicted from the bedroom and sent upstairs to sleep alone. He shuffles out of the room with his pillow, mumbling something about weak old women and their indulgence of children. "Oh *go,* Johann," Oma chastises him and turns her attention back to me where it belongs. I'm four or five, certainly not older than six; her comforter is easily twice my body weight. I can slip underneath it during hide-and-seek and not show so much as a bump to my pursuers.

"In Germany everyone sleeps under such a magnificent bed," I'm told. This one, in fact, had to be shipped special.

It's funny, really, the things she adjusts to, the things she does not. Her bedding will always be German, as will her garden and flowerbed, impossibly ornate and well-groomed while her American neighbors fuss over a couple of tomato plants, leaving them out to rot when the heat of July becomes just too much to deal with.

Like all good grandmothers she is unnecessarily patient with children. When the musical little twins from down the street walk by she calls them over and makes them sing a song for her. They claim they can't understand her accent, but

I think they're lying. They know her first as "the German lady" and eventually as Oma. She is everyone's Oma, the only Oma in Clarksville, a celebrity. My friend Lynn tried to call me there once but couldn't reach me because there was no "Oma" in the phone book.

◆   ◆   ◆

My father moved to the United States when he was nine. But my family's flirtation with American soil started a generation or two before that, when my great-great-grandfather mistakenly thought he'd killed someone in a bar fight. Nervous, he slipped over the Dutch border that same night and emigrated to Iowa, "where you can just spit on the ground and the corn grows three meters high!" He bought a farm there and lived quite contentedly for the rest of his life. Through a series of coincidences my Oma would eventually inherit this tract of land and move her husband and three children from their North Sea village to this foreign patch of prairie next to the Shell Rock River, where they would milk cows for nearly twenty years.

"One time we were down to just three dollars," she tells me. We are in the kitchen, where all our conversations take place. "And with that three dollars, I bought some bread." Of course. Bread, *Brot*, or—the diminutive—*Brötchen*, served at every meal, at the heart of every Lutheran prayer, synonymous with "money" in American English. She has an old wooden plaque hanging on the wall, giving thanks for *das Brot* in old German calligraphy, the same harsh script that I find in her heavy black Bible. *Bread.* How else would you spend your last three dollars?

"But it all worked out," she continues. "By the time we retired we had thirty cows." She says this with reverence, and it is clear this is an event, something not everyone could have done.

Assimilation was never a goal. My Opa never learned English well. He watched the midday agriculture reports, skimmed the local newspaper, and spoke little. He was content with hard work and good food, and his relationships with the rest of the family were often problematic, save for the attention he devoted to my little sister, whom he preferred over the rest of us.

Oma filled in the gaps. She taught herself English by reading children's books and watching soap operas. She kept wicked control over the household finances, which they tied up in land and more land, still nervous about saving paper money after living through the massive devaluation of the *Deutschmark*. She milked the cows, made hay, raised the kids, cooked every meal with an egg, a batch of flour and a glass of milk, and cleaned with a passion that could easily be labeled obsessive-compulsive.

"I'll have all the time in the world for you, Laury," she would tell me, "after I wash the dishes."

She thought labor-saving appliances were for wimps and did her laundry in a 1940s-era basin in the cellar. She has never owned a camera, stereo, dishwasher, or a remote control television set. When she moved to a new house she insisted that my father come over and install a rotary phone, since the existing push-button one was too decadent for her tastes. I am inclined to tease her—lightly—over her technology aversion until I remember that the money she saved through a lifetime of doing without helped put me and three cousins through college.

As I grew up, Oma and Opa were either intensely involved in my life or completely absent. They traveled back and forth from Germany to America nearly every year. They maintained households in both countries, had relatives in both countries, and lived pretty much the same in both countries: cooking, watching television, visiting family, and riding bicycles.

Both were born in villages outside Aurich. Aurich is located in Ostfriesland, a section of northern Germany strikingly similar to Iowa. It's farm country through and through, flat as a rug, dreary, gray, rainy, unbelievably clean, populated by innumerable white-haired children and their families, all of whom can trace their Ostfriesen ancestry back for centuries since no one moves to Ostfriesland voluntarily. If you live in Aurich it's because you were born there. The dominant language in this region is Low German, or *Plattdeutsch* (pronounced "platt dootch," or *pla'dootch* if you're in a hurry, but no one in Ostfriesland ever is). This was the language spoken at the Sunday dinner tables of my childhood, a hard language with lots of *hey's!* and *ho's!*, heavy on the consonants, sparse with anything that might require the delicate pursing of one's lips. It is a not a sensuous language, but a practical one, with many words related to farming techniques but not a single word for "love." And yet it is eminently emotional, the pitch of Platt rising and falling like the voice of an excited fisherman, rather than dry and controlled like standard German, the metronome of European tongues.

When I was about ten or eleven I learned to say "I can't *hear* my father's accent," rather than insisting that he didn't have one; the latter response inevitably elicited snickers. It was still hard to say. Admitting that my father's English was somehow tainted involved trusting others' opinions over my own empirical observations, as though I were a blind person stating authoritatively that my hair was blond even though I had never seen it myself. But I remember sitting in the backseat of a car in suburban Illinois with my cousin Heidi, waiting for our parents to drive us somewhere, and I decided to risk it. If anyone would tell me the truth, she would. "Does…my dad really have an accent?" I asked timidly.

She laughed at me outright. "Um, *duh.*" And then, more kindly, "What, you can't hear it?"

"No," I admitted.

She nodded. "I can't hear my mom's, either."

"Really?" I asked. *Are you nuts?* I thought. Tante Gerda's accent was obvious, dark and throaty, the kind American actresses emulate when they play Germans on TV.

"Kids can never hear their parents' accents," Heidi said matter-of-factly, as though this were common knowledge. Later she would grow up and get a graduate degree in linguistics.

Selective listening was apparently a common phenomenon. My mother claimed that my father had an accent when she met him, but he mysteriously lost it after they were married (some twenty years after he moved to America). Then, after their divorce when they spoke to each other less frequently, she insisted that he'd picked it up again. "I can barely understand him anymore," she said.

Of course she was joking, she knew that wasn't how it worked, but she, like I, had grown accustomed to thinking of him as The Standard Human, the default by which all others are compared. When I was growing up my dad served as my dictionary definition for the word "man," and if he rolled his r's, well then, all other men should, too. They were the ones in error, not him. That's how r is pronounced.

More trauma ensued when my German cousins told me he spoke German with an English accent. I couldn't hear that, either. But I remember that it depressed me. He couldn't win! And if *he* couldn't speak fluently in German—his native language—certainly I'd never be able to do it, either.

Yet it also intrigued me. He was nine when he moved to Iowa, about the age I was when my German cousins clued me in to the fact that my dad was really rather American. "He wears short pants," they pointed out (they meant cut-offs), "and he shoots animals" (i.e. goes hunting). I wasn't sure what to make of this. When I was with my American friends I'd grown accustomed to explaining away my family's idiosyncrasies by pointing to European traditions. The thought that my dad was weird everywhere was somewhat disconcerting.

Nor could I imagine moving to another country, right then, that summer, and eventually becoming so indoctrinated into another cultural tradition that I'd someday be unable to fit in with Americans if I tried.

That I might someday speak English with a foreign accent.

◆   ◆   ◆

I am going on twelve before I see Germany for the first time. I have never been away from my mother this long. Perhaps more importantly, I have never been alone with my father this long. Once my mother and sister leave the airport he becomes flustered, treats me like a distant niece who is visiting from out of state. We board the plane and he gives me the window seat. I've only flown once before, and that was just to Utah. While the more seasoned passengers chat, flip through magazines and struggle with their bulky carry-on luggage, I listen intently to the pilot's safety instructions. *Your seat cushion can also be used as a flotation device.* Really! How cool! Because I am eleven, I hope desperately that the plane will crash.

The stewardesses—they weren't "flight attendants" back then—are all heavily made up and smell good. They slink up and down the aisles, bowing and smiling, flashing row upon row of shockingly white teeth. Coming from farm country I'm used to seeing women covered in cowshit. These stewardesses seem ethereal to me, like walking mannequins, not quite human. (Several years later I would run out of tampons mid-flight and ask a stewardess if she has one, thinking they have such things on board the way they carry diapers and vegetarian dinners. They don't. However, she does have one in her purse and discreetly hands it over. It's pencil-thin, Slender Regular, the kind of tampon that is only advertised on the back pages of magazines catering to prepubescent girls who worry that using Tampax will interfere with their virginity. This little straw of a tampon lasts all of fifteen minutes and further confirms my belief that stewardesses are not real people.)

Seven long hours later we land in Amsterdam and are greeted by my uncle Ray, a Wisconsin native who married my Tante Meta and has lived in Germany for over a decade. The first thing I notice are the license plates on his car: no-nonsense black on white, with entirely too many letters to be practical for law enforcement purposes. I want to write to my friends immediately and tell them of this discovery.

The second thing I notice are the bathrooms, which confuse me. We stop at an off-road bathroom with a toilet that flushes by pulling a chain that hangs from the ceiling rather than by pushing a lever on the toilet itself. *How foreign*, I think, my mind suddenly filled with images of millions of Dutch people pooping.

Eventually we wave our American passports at the customs officials and, suddenly, myth becomes reality. We are in Germany, the real Germany, the country which I had begun to doubt even existed. To me it looks as much like The Netherlands as Iowa looks like Nebraska. But I don't say this out loud. We keep driving. Up and around the countryside, speeding along the Autobahn where there are no speed limits. My uncle has a tendency to drive like he speaks—that is, slowly—but it is nonetheless a dizzying pace for me, accustomed as I am to the 55mph laws of American interstates. I press my forehead against the glass. Everything is strange: the billboards (in a foreign language!), the street lights, so many bicycles, so many trains. The houses are too neat and too close together. Even the dotted lines on the road separating the lanes of highway are the wrong length. My uncle manipulates the traffic remarkably well. I forget that he is American.

Soon the houses thin out and are replaced by forest, farms, and cows. The landscape flattens. The rooftops, once brown and red and black, are now uniformly orange. And after some slowing, turning, and bumping we finally stop in front of a two-story brick house on the corner of a narrow cobblestone road with a brick driveway and a well-manicured hedge. And there is my Oma, wearing her ever-familiar blue dress and white apron, running towards us, arms outstretched. My Opa is behind her. We've arrived.

Around the house and up the back steps, my father, my uncle, and my Opa carry our suitcases. But Oma concerns herself only with me, pushing me into the kitchen and heaping potatoes—already cooked and waiting on the stove, of course—onto my plate. How was your trip? How is your mother? How is *das kleine Lischen*—my sister Lisa, who is only four and is missed with a vengeance.

Oma and Opa own this house but, because they travel back and forth so much, they live in the tiny upstairs apartment ("under the rafters," my Opa says dryly) and rent out the bottom story to a young couple. (Oma says they are married but I find out later that they are not. This means two things: one, they are typically German, living together through an extraordinarily long engagement, and two, Oma likes them enough to pretend that they are not living in sin—if only to herself, since they, being young and modern, show no embarrassment over their situation.)

The upstairs apartment has two bedrooms (one for Oma and Opa, one for me), a kitchen, a bathroom, and a living room, where my father sleeps on a mattress on the floor. Every room, even the kitchen, has a door that closes with a lever rather than a doorknob. I fiddle with these levers constantly, savoring their exoticism. (In fact I still have an urge to do this whenever I am in Germany, but now that I am an adult I manage to repress it.) The living room furniture is not so different from what I am used to, and the beds I recognize from being at Oma's house in America. She has featherbeds here, too, and just like in Iowa she has two single beds strapped together rather than a double bed. This is apparently a common custom, but I still don't understand its origins. There are no closets. Clothes are kept in giant *Schranks*—floor-to-ceiling wardrobes that inevitably take up a good part of the room. More modern homes often have one bedroom wall entirely covered by the interlocking cupboards, dressers and mirrors of a common designer, but Oma, being frugal even by German standards, has accumulated a motley crüe of beds, blankets, end tables and *Schranks* over the years, and her hybrid collection has simply been split evenly between the two bedrooms. Everything is wood, however, so it doesn't look as bad as one might think.

Outside, Germany is not like I imagined it. For one thing, unlike those pictures we received every year from my aunt and uncle, the country is in color rather than black and white. The children don't wear dirndl dresses and lederhosen; they wear jeans and sweatshirts just like me. There is no trace of the Von Trapp children anywhere.

What Germany *was* filled with was other Omas. Millions of them. Throw a stone anywhere in Germany and you'll hit an Oma with her gray hair pulled back in a bun, carrying fresh fruit and baguettes back from the market on her bicycle.

And suddenly, my own Oma's actions all fall into place. Her fussing over my failure to clean my plate, her constant attempts to foist a banana off on me every time I leave the house, the way she talks to children she doesn't know, even the way she gasps—sucking in her breath and throwing her hands in the air—all of these actions are common here among women of her station in life.

My second day in Aurich I am visited by a group of neighbor girls, approximately my age, who have heard that I was coming. They march up the back steps and into Oma's kitchen; she knows them all by name and serves them chocolates, tea, and cookies. They chat.

Chat.

In fluent German, sometimes *Plattdeutsch*, laughing and poking each other, gulping their tea and answering her questions about their mothers and who they're related to and where they live. I understand the flow of the conversation, more or less, but cannot participate, because I do not share their mother tongue.

They are *chatting* with my Oma.

They are doing something I have never done.

I talk to my Oma, of course, but our conversations have always been stilted, hampered by the gaps in our language skills. By the time I was five years old I was used to speaking loudly and clearly with my grandparents, refining my vocabulary to make it comprehensible to their foreign ears. Some things I knew would be impossibly difficult to explain, and these things were simply never discussed. Our conversations were slow, accompanied by exaggerated hand gestures and interspersed with Germanisms. I had, of course, heard Oma speak naturally with my father, with my grandfather, with other relatives, with her elderly Ostfriesen friends. But never with anyone my age.

Even more startling is the fact that they seem so comfortable with her. I don't have to explain her to them the way I do with my friends in America, tell them that she understands this but not that, assure them that calling someone "plump" is considered a compliment in her country. These girls, these authentic German girls, need no such explanations. They understand my Oma better than I do. They have Omas of their own. They know how these things go.

And I realize with a start that I've spent my whole life viewing Oma through a sort of science fiction lens, one that required the suspension of disbelief for the story to make sense. In America she was like an actor dressed in Elizabethan garb, confused in the middle of a disco, reciting sonnets while surrounded by girls in tight jeans and hipsters smoking cigarettes. Suddenly the disco had been whisked away and a 16th-century backdrop slammed down in its place, complete with other actors who also speak in iambic pentameter. With the help of an accommodating context, she became downright ordinary.

◆   ◆   ◆

During my second year of college I went home to visit my American grandfather, who asked me what I was learning down there in Iowa City.

"The politics behind mechanized farming in Sierra Leone," I deadpanned. It was true: I'd read a paper on that very topic the night before.

Grandpa pondered this. "Well, good," he said, chuckling. "I was worried you weren't learning *anything*."

Oh, the melodrama that could have been averted had both sides of my family seen humor in the esoteric. My mom's parents hadn't needed college to make a living, but hell, if you want to go, no one's stopping you.

Contrast the simplicity of that exchange with the nightmare that ensued when I was fifteen and my Oma's sister, Tante Hanni, asked me what my cousin Heidi was studying. I knew it was communications, but not knowing the German word for that (which, I later learned, is "communications"), I proceeded to give a torturous definition involving radios, television, writing—I didn't know the word for "public relations" so I had to leave that out—

"Proten," I finally concluded. Yes. Heidi is studying talking.

Tante Hanni allowed me this insane detour, then asked what was really her only interest: could Heidi be a teacher with that or not?

"Well, no," and more with the radios and the talking.

Aiyy! Was it too late to switch??

Here one must note that of Tante Hanni's five grandchildren, two were enmeshed in the German system of higher education, which has no tradition of liberal arts. Future doctors study medicine and medicine alone; teachers study only education. My cousin Gesa had begun with biology and then economics before switching to teaching; this was an ordeal, since Germany's publicly funded university system doesn't allow for much meandering deviation. Electives can't retroactively become core classes as they can in America, so a year spent in the wrong field is a year entirely wasted.

As it turned out Heidi did eventually change her major (to German) and still managed to complete her degree in four years. She even became a teacher for a while before going into the more lucrative field of technical writing. But none of that was in the cards as I was having my discussion with Tante Hanni, and she was completely distraught at the thought of her granddaughter spending all that money on a degree—for in America one has to pay for such things—without coming out of it with the one solid thing she knew college-educated girls could always fall back on: a teacher's certificate.

My Oma would have similar conversations with me. The Sierra-Leone-mechanized-farming joke would have gone right over her head. "Yes, but what can you *do* with it?" would be the real, the only, question. And while my American grandpa clearly wondered the same thing, he wondered it the way he wondered if there was boxing on television tonight and whether there was still any milk in the refrigerator. Oma, on the other hand, would lose sleep, come down with nervous chills and fevers, and rearrange her financial investments in order to account for the fact that at least one of her granddaughters—and, *Gott im Himmel,* the way it was looking some days possibly all of them—were going to end up in the poorhouse with all this talk of French minors and "political science" and delusions of becoming professional musicians (an oxymoron if there ever was one). When my cousin Gunda finally did get her teaching certification I, for one, slept better at night, if only because I knew that Oma's worry burden had been momentarily lightened. Of course shortly thereafter the chorus became "if Gundi can do it, you can, too."

The heart of all this, naturally, is security. Teachers work for the government, and landing a government job in Germany is like returning to the womb. Government workers get a good salary, with benefits, liberal time off, and, barring atrocious abuses such as setting one's students on fire during fifth period, *a teacher can never be fired.* Thus government work, for anyone who's had a passing exposure to the insecurity that comes with war and starvation, is the occupational equivalent of the Holy Grail. Land a government job and you're set for life. In America this would induce panic—*set for life?? you mean I have to do the same thing every day until I die??*—but in Germany it's cause for celebration. Our days of stress and angst about tomorrow are over! Hallelujah.

My father has no patience for this. Europe's social benefits and 36-hour work weeks and overly long vacations piss him off, and having to listen to Germans' complaints about their struggles with their free health plan or their indecision over where to go for the summer (Majorca or Brazil?) just make it all the more intolerable. He'd rather be back in the local tavern in Clarksville, surrounded by farmers, men who know how to generate capital, men who know how to run a business, men who *work* for a living. Recently he pointed out that he and my uncle Garrelt, a dairy farmer, were the only ones in the family who contributed to the economy. "The rest of you"—teachers, students, civil servants, nonprofit workers, religious leaders—"are all sucking off the tit of the system."

Americans pay lip service to job security, especially after a stock market crash, but they don't fetishize it as Germans do. The American nightmare is being tied down, being immobile. My sister spent three years living in her car.

Americans are by their very nature transients. I have difficulty celebrating this, believing as I do that we *should* have a socialized health care system, that job security *should* be a right, that family ties *do* bind tighter than any other—in other words I believe, on some abstract level, that *permanence* is the root that folds humans together as a community. This is my Eastern Hemisphere side talking, even if it's the Eastern Hemisphere side my Eastern Hemispherean father rejected.

And yet on some other, subconscious level I understand that the ultimate freedom is the freedom to flee.

◆   ◆   ◆

My dad once told me that he was looking forward to school until he realized that only the top stratum of the *Zuckertüte* held candy. Below that it was layered with worthless tissue paper. Nice trick there, eh? My illusions of Germany were similarly shattered when I finally arrived there myself, and later, as I learned more about history and politics, my childhood vision of America as a perfectly-crafted project would also wear thin. But stories of immigration and emigration will never bore me, nor will stories of creating a life within a particular cultural backdrop, particularly when the speaker is a newcomer and takes nothing for granted.

When I was fifteen, in Rahe, a village outside of Aurich, I babbled on to my cousin Gesa about wanting to go to Austria, to Italy, to Egypt, to Scotland. I have no idea why I'd be dreaming of travel in Rahe, when the village defined geographical perfection to me both then and now. If anything I was irritated with those who lived there but didn't appreciate it. But I was fifteen, and therefore fickle.

"You know the word *heimweh*?" Gesa asked, and I nodded. I'd confronted that word a million times since arriving in Germany: *"Hast du Heimweh?"* the relatives would ask me over and over again—*"Are you homesick?"*

"The Germans have an opposite word," Gesa said, *"fernweh*, which means the desire to travel."

"Fern" means distant and *"weh"* means pain, and I sensed immediately that *"fernweh"* was not a craving for adventure, but, like homesickness in reverse, a *longing*, a need to get out, a sort of nostalgia for the future.

Some eight years later my husband and I were on my father's farm back in Iowa, making last-minute arrangements to leave for Egypt with our baby daughter. My father-in-law had just died in Cairo and we needed to leave as soon as possible. Oma was beside herself with angst. Why leave America? The good America? *Tja!* Going to Germany was okay, that was home just like Iowa was, but to Egypt? A truly foreign country? What would become of us, taking a baby to the desert, so far away from family and everything familiar?

My dad, I could tell, had enlisted her help in laying on the guilt trip. Just back from a trip to Germany, he was in appreciate-America mode himself and didn't want us to leave, but emotional pleas were something he'd always left to the women in the family. Oma rattled off a rapid-fire litany of worries, stresses over making a living and the ever-imminent threat of war in the Middle East. I was leaning against the car, bags already packed, saying whatever I could think of to make it seem okay that I was disappearing to North Africa and taking her great-grandchild with me.

Was she persuaded by my arguments? I'm not sure. Probably not. She's rarely been persuaded by anything but the force of her own experience. But in the end that's all that mattered. My Opa had died just two years earlier and I think she was remembering him.

"I know," she finally said, forgiving me. "When we were young we left our homeland, too."

◆   ◆   ◆

"We of the here and now are not for a moment hedged in the time-world, nor confined with it. We are incessantly flowing over and over to those who preceded us, to our origins and to those who seemingly come after us."

—*Selected Letters of Rainer Maria Rilke*

Germany the Way I Remember It

By Gerda Taylor

Moments come and go…sunshine and golden laughter…pale gray days and rain…and mostly I do not recognize them for what they are…my life.

I had been waiting patiently for my appointment with the nationalization office in Chicago. The testing in American History and Government for foreigners wanting to become citizens of the United States was being held in the Dirksen Building on Dearborn Street in Chicago. The date for my test came in the mail today.

This true story takes you back to the year 1942 in my hometown of Wiesens, West Germany.

◆　　　◆　　　◆

It was summer and Germany was at war. Our home was in Wiesens, in northern Germany. My mother, alarmed and frightened by sirens, pulled my brother and me out of our small beds. She calmly wrapped some blankets around us and somehow managed to answer our urgent questions. Her hands moved quickly as she placed us in a room near a thick wall and away from windows. Already several stray bullets had entered the house; luckily no one got hurt.

A road was the only thing that separated our house from the canal which held the main transportation. It was a great target for *Tiefflieger* (low-flying planes). Ships carrying war materials came through on a regular basis. Every now and then our house was mistaken for one of those ships.

Even though danger was all around us, my brother and I loved to ride on the bridge. A bridge attendant had to be present to open the gates. A senior citizen from the neighborhood and a good friend of the family was in charge of this drawbridge, now that our father had been called away to the battle fields.

One time I dared to be on the open bridge all by myself. Suddenly the skies were black with *Tieffliegern* and the adults had no choice but to go for cover. There I was, standing all alone on the open bridge with no one to protect me and no place to escape. I just stood there screaming. It took only minutes before the planes passed, the bridge was closed, and my mother reached for me to calm me down. Those few minutes of intense fear, however, had called my small body to become totally stiff. I was only four years old.

Krieg (war) was a nasty word which we children often heard but didn't understand. To us it meant the fear that we saw in the eyes of adults. They figured out that the enemy was near, and we wanted to know why. We had lots of questions for which there were no easy answers. The name "Hitler" came up often.

And so it was that because of Adolf Hitler, young men under the age of twenty were called to fight for their *Vaterland*. The war seemed to be coming to an end, and Hitler, at all costs, hung on to his insane idea to win the war.

One Saturday my Aunt Netti came to visit. We were having tea when we heard sirens and shortly thereafter received word that there were wounded people on one of the boats. We all walked along the canal, sometimes having to go for cover in a ditch because of another warning siren, until we arrived at the boat. My brave aunt went across the unstable planks that someone had quickly erected. She went inside with the help of the bridge attendant, and the wounded were carried out quickly and brought to our house.

One young man looked to be about eighteen years of age. I remember watching his face as my mother frantically searched for first aid materials. He never uttered a word when she tried to stop the bleeding with a handmade tourniquet. The Red Cross wagon came soon thereafter to take him and the other soldiers to the hospital. I overheard one of the grown-ups say that the young boy would probably lose one of his legs.

I sat quietly for a long time, looking at the blood that had dripped onto our wooden, coal-heated foot warmer. This picture and the blank expression on the young boy's face stayed with me a long time.

We must have had happy times in this secluded area, surrounded by nature—our childhood home. I cannot remember much of it…

We knew that food would eventually be rationed. So, out of necessity, we turned to underhanded, forbidden ways, such as burying groceries. We buried huge white cotton bags filled with flour, sugar, dried vegetables, and tea. We buried the bags under the floor of our barn, and outside with a tree planted on top.

No one would suspect. My brother and I knew what was going on, but we were smart enough by now to never mention it.

German soldiers came around to plan strategies to keep the enemy from advancing too far. We got used to seeing mines, guns, and armed soldiers. One day my brother was at the front of the house when a German soldier shouted to him that the bridge was going to be blown up! Even though my brother was only five years old, he knew that this message had to be told to my mother immediately. My mother quickly reached for some important papers and rushed us out of the house. We ran to a neighbor's house about two kilometers away. When we returned we saw that all of the windows in our home needed to be replaced. The job of blowing up the bridge, however, was only half done.

My mother became very angry at the soldiers who appeared to be drinking alcohol. They were probably fed up with what was being asked of them. It was a hopeless situation; the war was coming to an end and it could not be won.

My mother made her disapproval known to the group of German soldiers when one of them came after her shouting, *"Ich shiesse Sie tot!"*—*I am going to kill you!* She quickly ran inside the house and down the stairs, where she remembered our hiding place. Only the immediate family knew about this. The soldier frantically searched the house from top to bottom and then gave up, slowly lowering his gun.

Oh that I had the wings of a dove! I would hurry to my place of shelter, far from the tempest and storm (Psalm 55:6, 8)

And He whispered to my heart…it's alright, it's alright…

◆   ◆   ◆

Eventually the war ended, and we counted twenty-one bullet holes in the walls of our home. We were spared. What we had experienced was minimal compared to those Germans whose cities burned to the ground.

Germany had lost the Second World War!

British soldiers in nice uniforms came to help us load our belongings into their army trucks. We had to move many kilometers away, to the home of our grandparents. The political party my father had belonged to was no longer in existence. The house we had lived in during the war had to be given up. Where was our father? He had been serving in the Navy in the port Kiel in West Germany. Was he now held captive in Russia?

The Postwar Years

A very new and different life began for us.

My grandparents owned a small dairy farm on which they had to work very hard to keep earning a living. Except for the war years, my grandparents had lived a relatively normal life. One daughter (Tante Netti to us children) was still unmarried and living at home. The arrival of my mother, my brother, and myself did not make them very happy. We became a disruption in their daily lives. Unfortunately we needed to stay with them for a long time.

My mother decided to become a midwife. This was something she had dreamed of, and the need to support her children became the incentive to follow her dream. She had no formal education, but now needed to go back to school at age thirty!

My mother was aboard the first running train in that northern part of Germany which headed toward a city called Celle. The train had no windows. It was packed with soldiers returning to their homes and fugitives trying to reach their destinations.

It was very difficult for my mother to leave her children in the care of her sister and parents, but the training she needed took two years. We still had not gotten word from my father and his whereabouts.

◆   ◆   ◆

Those families who had extra room in their homes were ordered to take in fugitives. Russia had invaded parts of Germany such as Ostpreussen. Many families, in order to escape the brutality of the Russian soldiers, decided to flee into the heartland of Germany. My grandparents offered their home to such a family, a mother with two children. They had been traveling for weeks without a change of fresh clothing, money, or much food to eat. They were dirty, their hair was full of lice, and they brought to us a contagious disease called *Kretze*. *Kretze* was a terrible skin rash, the result of poor nourishment.

To this day I can remember the stench of the horrible salve, Mitigall, which was the only medication available to relieve the terrible itching.

Of course my brother and I caught the disease. Our arms and legs were covered with the rash, and the horrible constant smell of the Mitigall just had to be endured. Our cousin and playmate came around every day. The doors, however, remained locked until everyone in the house became well again.

My Tante Netti took over the responsibility of raising us. She was very strict, but as much as we disliked that, we admitted later that she taught us many things which prepared us for the unknown still ahead of us.

◆   ◆   ◆

Most children are brought to school by a parent, especially on their first day. I was taken to school by a soldier whose name was Arnulf. He had remained with us on his return from the war. My Tante Netti fell in love with him and the two were married. Since some of our local teachers had not returned from the war, my new Onkel Arnulf was hired by the school board and now taught third grade. What a surprise!

Each day we walked a long way to school, rain or shine. There were bicycles on my grandparents' farm, but they were only used for farm purposes. Parts for repairs were not on the market; my grandfather fixed everything, and we all learned to be very frugal with equipment that we owned.

On one of those days, on the way home from school, something happened that left me frightened of walking that same route ever again!

I was walking with a friend and, as usual, was taking my time. I was never eager to do the chores that were waiting for me at home. I decided to climb a gate to a farmer's field, when I suddenly heard a faint cry. I jumped down and took a closer look. To my amazement I saw tiny hands reaching out from under sod and leaves!

It was a baby! A tiny, newborn baby! I ran as fast as I possibly could to the home of my Tante Hilda and Onkel Johann. My aunt followed me to the place where I had seen the baby. She carefully lifted it up, brushed off the dirt and leaves, and wrapped it in her apron.

She took the baby home and gave it a bottle of formula that had been prepared for her own baby. The *Polizei* (police) were contacted and shortly thereafter they arrived together with the Red Cross. The infant was taken to a nearby hospital.

Later we were told that the mother gave birth on her own. She was only sixteen and afraid to let her parents know she was pregnant. The father was a soldier. I didn't realize until I was much older that I had perhaps saved this baby's life!

◆   ◆   ◆

In the town of Wiesens, where we had lived during the war, we didn't have the opportunity to play with other children. Wiesens was a small town and somewhat isolated. Because of this lack of experience with playmates, we believed whatever the kids in our new neighborhood told us. We had no idea that children could be cruel and uncaring.

While strolling through the fields one day, we came across a chain of bullets. A couple of neighborhood boys convinced my unsuspecting brother, eight years old at the time, that it might be fun to play war and make some bullets go off by hitting them with a rock. Even though some of us, including my cousin, knew that this was dangerous, we did nothing. We made sure that we took cover near a hill; then we waited…

Be devoted to one another in brotherly love. (Romans 12:10)

By and far, it is those things that I've left undone that rob me of my serenity. If only I had taken time to listen…make a call…say a prayer…and then I am reminded—there's today.

My brother lifted the rock and came down on the chain of bullets with all his might. I heard the noises of the shot and then the scream! Within seconds I was by his side and I saw the blood rushing from his forehead and wrist. A bullet had grazed his hand and also entered his head. People came rushing from everywhere.

My brother was rushed to the hospital. He was hurt badly, but lived by a miracle. The bullet did not touch his eye.

Hospitals were still very overcrowded, and two days later Garrelt came home, heavily bandaged. I became painfully aware—and was reminded during each day of his recovery—of what I had let happen.

◆   ◆   ◆

Two years passed and we got used to living in the home of my grandparents, who were very hard-working people. My grandmother ruled the house, and everyone, including my mother, had to follow her instructions. My grandfather was a very quiet man. He just did his work and asked very little of life. He had served in World War I and received the highest honor a soldier could receive.

My mother returned from her two-year schooling, certified and ready to help deliver babies. Tante Netti became pregnant, and when her time came to deliver her nine-pound daughter, it took three days and three nights. I can still hear her cries, since my bedroom was not far from where my cousin Dagmar was born. There was only one doctor in the area and very little medication available. My mother never left her sister's side and thus had one of her first experiences as a new midwife.

But it seemed there had to be more obstacles put in the way of "normal" living. The Nazis, obviously, were not among favored memories. Anyone even slightly suspected of being connected to past evils had to go through what was called *Entnazifizierung*. It was like a cleansing of connections with certain political parties. My father had been in the German Navy in one of the well-known ports called Kiel in West Germany. Later he belonged to Hilter's Elite.

A lot of papers had to be produced and forms filled out to prove that my mother had nothing to do with the Nazis. While she did what was in her power to establish a right to start her career, German authorities did what they could to make it impossible for her.

◆   ◆   ◆

Already before the war began and until the time Germany lost, Adolf Hitler was strongly against organized religion. Families were not permitted to have Bibles, hymnals, or any Christian books in their homes. He ordered these books to be burned. During his reign and while leading Germany into destruction, he also took away the right to Holy Baptism.

My brother and I were baptized in 1947 by an ordained pastor at the Lamberti Kirche in Aurich.

Our confirmation happened under more normal circumstances. Religion was part of our daily curriculum now. Confirmation classes were taught on Saturdays at the same church in Aurich. It was customary to frame one's baptismal and confirmation certificates and hang them where they could be seen and read by visitors.

All of us who have been baptized into Jesus Christ were baptized into His death. Therefore, we have been buried with Him by baptism into death, so that, just as Christ was raised from the dead by the Glory of the Father, so we too might walk in the newness of life. (Romans 6:3, 4)

My parents got divorced. The reason for the divorce is unclear to me; I like to think it was war-related. My mother, my brother, and I continued living in the home of my grandparents until the summer of 1954. My father went back to East Germany. He married the widow of a *Kriegskamerad* (war associate), whose death he had witnessed. His friend had left behind a wife and four daughters.

My mother and I moved to the town of Aurich in 1954. My brother was needed on the farm and agreed to remain with our grandparents. My mother had saved enough money to buy a piece of land and have a small house built on it. I was very excited! I could hardly wait to get away from my grandmother. For a long time my secret wish had been to have a place of my own where only my mother and I ruled. It turned out to be the happiest year of my life.

When I was sixteen I found a job where I learned bookkeeping skills and other business practices. My mother had become very popular and helped deliver countless babies. I was able to do all of her bookkeeping.

◆   ◆   ◆

While riding my bicycle to work one day, I noticed a man following me. Once he caught up with me, he passed me and sped away. This continued to happen almost every day. Sometimes I would spot him in my favorite grocery store. He would already be there, only to disappear again. I didn't know what to make of this strange behavior, so I just laughed about it. Then one day he rang our doorbell and when my mother answered, began to play his violin for us. She, too, thought he was very strange. We did enjoy the music, however.

I had changed jobs and was now employed at the *Sozialgericht*, a government office where senior citizens whose documents were lost or burned during the war had a chance to claim their hard-earned *Rente* (social security benefits).

One day, when preparing the courtroom for that day's hearings, I noticed the same man who had been following me seated in the room. I went upstairs, somewhat shaken, and explained to our judge about the visitor and why it made me so nervous. Judge Roever immediately asked him to leave the building and never to show up again! The stranger explained to the judge that he wanted to witness first-hand how I handled myself as a court reporter. Why…?

Well, the hearings began and while listening to the unique hardships of these senior citizens, I forgot my own troubles and was able to concentrate on my work.

But the stranger, whose name we now knew to be Friedrich, was not ready to give up on whatever it was he was after. He continued to follow me.

During the following week I was given a note by a co-worker. It was from my father, who had come back from East Germany to settle in the nearby town of Walle. Apparently one of his war buddies worked in the same office as I did. I was confused when I read the note: "Meet me at the Hotel Piquerhof in Aurich on Wednesday after work." After discussing the message with my mother, I decided to go to the meeting.

The hotel owner, a woman and also a friend of my father's, greeted me at the main door and invited me to come upstairs to her private tea room. The table was set with fine linen and beautiful china, ready for afternoon tea. While I was waiting, the hostess spoke favorably of my father and also about the fact that he missed me very much—a set-up, I realized later. I was very nervous, wondering what my father was up to.

Soon he appeared. He was not alone, however. To my great surprise, I saw the man who had been following me, the one who had so boldly come into my place of work to inquire about me.

Now that I had a chance to have a closer look at him I realized that he was about forty-five years old. I was only twenty. My anxiety escalated. I could hardly contain myself. Everyone sat down, and we were offered tea and dainty pastry. I certainly was not interested in anything other than what was expected of me.

I remember feeling my heart pound when my father looked directly at me and began to speak. "This is Friedrich," he began. "He is a good friend of mine. Friedrich is able to get my job back for me. He has great influence with the right people and can assure that my old government position will be returned to me. I will then be comfortable for the rest of my life. Wouldn't that be wonderful, Gerdi?"

I nodded.

"All Friedrich wants," he continued, "is to marry you. He is very much in love with you. The engagement should happen right away."

All at once I understood that my father was ready to trade my life for his old government job. What about me? Did I count? The anger rose up in me—I felt nauseated—and I jumped up and left. My father tried to stop me: "Please hear me out," he pleaded with me.

I raced home as fast as my legs would allow me, and upon seeing my mother, I burst into tears of anger and disappointment. "My own father..." was all that I could say. My mother was very understanding. She listened and then mumbled something about how war experiences can change people. I was grateful to have a mother as strong as mine.

◆   ◆   ◆

Four years later I applied for the necessary papers needed to immigrate to the United States. I found a sponsor family that lived in Evanston, Illinois. My aunt, uncle, and cousins had also moved to America. My great-grandmother had died and she had willed her land and other property to them. My plan was to stay a year or two near my aunt and uncle.

I was twenty-four years old when I got off of the plane at O'Hare International Airport in Chicago. My cousin, who now lived in Iowa, came to greet me.

A new journey in a foreign country began that day...

Hinrike and Garrelt Fecht have been running a dairy farm in Rahe, a village outside Aurich, for more than thirty years. Rahe is famous in Osfriesland for its "Upstalsboom," a tree on a small hill where Frisians held meetings to make and enforce local laws during the Middle Ages. This time period is known as the "Friesische Freiheit" (Frisian freedom); it was a period when the Frisians fiercely maintained their independence from European feudalism.

Any visitor to the Fechts' kitchen remembers it as a special place, a place where the pace is both slow and hectic at the same time and everyone is relaxed and generous toward one another. Garrelt and Riki have been married since she was just eighteen and their teamwork is legendary in the family. Since they're dairy farmers, their lives usually revolve around the milking schedule. But I remember one day, when I was fifteen, Riki had to go to a funeral that unexpectedly kept her away from the house for a few hours. This was one of the few occasions in which the structure of the day was thrown off course. At about 12:15 Onkel Garrelt came into the living room and asked me very politely if I knew how to cook. I said that no, unfortunately, I didn't. "Ja," he said, "me neither." Everyone in the house wandered around a bit aimlessly until

Tante Riki appeared an hour later, breathless. She had the tea on the stove before she'd even take off her jacket.

~Laura Fokkena

A New World

By Habbo Fokkena

Bremerhafen, March 1956

I am standing on a dock, on a typical gray, rainy day in northern Germany, waiting to board the passenger liner that will take my family and me to Amerika. Not to Canada, North America, nor the United States, but Amerika. To one leaving, it is always Amerika. We do not distinguish.

I am nine years of age. My sister Meta is fifteen, and my brother Willie (Wilhelm, but we never called him that) is three. My father is forty-five and my mother is thirty-nine. What possessed them to transplant all of us to another country where they do not even speak the language is beyond me. But, at age nine, I do not think of such things. My thoughts are focused on the present, on the rain, the ship, the tearful relatives around us, and the North Sea. Across from us is the big ship, the *Bremen*, waiting to receive us. I have never seen such a large vessel. It is huge and foreboding.

Some of my relatives have come along to say goodbye, and we take pictures. The adults know what saying goodbye means. For the vast majority of Ostfriesens who left their homeland, there was no *Wiedersehn*. They left for good and never came back. Contact was reduced to the obligatory Christmas letter. The adults know this, and the goodbyes are heartfelt.

My goodbye had come from my class and my beloved teacher, Fraulein Schneemann. She had been with us since we started school and I'd never known another teacher. She, unbeknownst to me, organized a goodbye sendoff on my last day of school. In typical German fashion, it included little handmade cards and several songs. As I stood in front of the class, with her arm around me, I realized for the first time that this trip must be something major, and started tearing. But her arm around me and a quick word convinced me that boys do not cry at such occasions. I don't remember what they sang, or the names of most of my classmates, but I do remember that goodbye.

At home there was packing to do, visits from the neighbors, and goodbyes from my grandparents. We first stayed one or two nights in a town an hour or two away, where most of my father's relatives lived. I had to sleep in an unfamiliar bed. But I did get to see a movie with my cousin Helmut. He says it was Prince Eisenherz, a story of knightly deeds and castles. I do not recall that, except by the telling.

I do remember the drive in a Mercedes to Bremerhafen. A Mercedes was a big deal to us, a kingly conveyance, and I was proud to ride in it. But mostly I remember the rain, a dripping kind of rain that is characteristic of Germany.

But on the dock in Bremerhafen I'm not thinking of leaving Walle, the small village that has been my life since my birth. I'm not thinking of Amerika, either: that I can't understand the language, that I have no idea of what school will be like, or where I will live. Instead, my thoughts are focused on what will happen next. We finally board the ship and find our cabin. We return to the deck, wave frantically, and the ship slowly drifts into the North Sea. For the next five or six days, it will be our home.

We end up in a small family cabin tucked below the decks, with a tiny bathroom. It has a porthole, and being a boy, I get the bunk where I can look out of it. But there is little to see on this trip. The sea is gray, full of huge rolling waves, and we have gulls following us the entire trip.

The ship itself is far more interesting. Some of my family members are seasick and have to stay in the cabin. My father and I are not. He's used to this, having sailed the seven seas as a young man. He has regaled me with tales of crossing the equator, and King Neptune. He still has a large seaman's tattoo on his arm, which I have admired frequently. It's a typical sailor's tattoo, full of ropes, mermaids, and anchors. In Amerika, as he becomes a farmer, it will fade under his farmer's tan. But in northern Germany it's still prominent. One doesn't tan in Walle.

Ship life is exciting for a young boy. I'm given free rein to roam, and take advantage. One night I discover the movie theater and stay late, sitting by the steps, to see a movie. It is free, and has adult content I do not fully understand. When I return to the cabin, I immediately discover that I'm in trouble. I hadn't told my parents where I went and they have been looking all over the ship for me. They react with typical parental anger, relief, and scolding, and put me promptly to bed. In the future, my freedom is restricted.

Meals come in shifts, and again I cause my parents distress. I'm used to my mother's common German foods. Eating out isn't something we do. The ship board food is foreign, and in spite of the threats and cajoling of my parents, I eat very little. The poor steward tries, but without success. I remain a picky eater, a habit I won't lose until I'm in the military. Nevertheless, I manage to survive the trip.

Arriving in Amerika

The Statue of Liberty is the symbol of freedom. For years it has welcomed immigrants from all over the world. In 1956, it welcomed the Fokkena family. We had finally arrived in the land of the free, the land of opportunity. Yet, to a nine-year-old boy, none of this is important.

Instead, I'm excited to land and leave the ship. We had already landed once, in Halifax, but I didn't get to go ashore. Our future is not in Canada, but in the United States.

Passengers comment on the statue, but not about the freedom she symbolized. Instead, I remember a joke about whether she ever gets tired of holding up her arm. The joke was fitting, for I'd soon learn that Amerika was indeed about freedom, but it was also about hard work and sore arms.

But she is magnificently large. Even larger are the skyscrapers of New York. Never in my life have I seen such enormous buildings. They are huge. We travel through canyons of steel that appear to fall over on us.

The people also fascinate me. We're transported to the railroad station in a taxi, my first one. Even more impressively, the taxi is driven by a black man, the first I have ever seen.

We do not communicate with our driver. He doesn't know German, and we don't speak English. Only my sister, who has had at least one or two years of English in school, can say a few words, and she is drafted to speak for us. I notice she doesn't speak English as well as we think she does—my father has to try to make the driver understand what we want. Luckily the driver, having no doubt seen this before, knows where to take us.

We spend the next day on the train. I don't recall much of that trip. Maybe I slept, or was suffering from information overload. But I do remember arriving in Chicago. Again, we are in a huge city. But this time we are not lost, since we're met by old acquaintances of my parents, neighbors from a nearby village back in Germany who now live in Chicago.

We stay in their house for at least one night. They, to show off Chicago, take us out to eat at a German restaurant. It looks impressive, but to the picky eater in the Fokkena family it's all a waste. It's not my mother's food.

But it's comforting to hear Low German again. I can understand everything being said and the pattern of conversation is familiar. I like Chicago.

The familiarity ends as we resume our journey westward. Again it is by train, Rockford, Dubuque, Waterloo, and then, finally, Butler County, Iowa. We end up in the home of one of our three sponsors, Nanne Franken. He, too, is German, speaks our language, but has been here for many years. His Low German, like most of the people who have lived here for years, is interspersed with strange words like *barn, corn, courthouse, sales barn, beans,* and *cultivator*. They have crept unnoticed into the language and now reside there as if they have always been there. In a few years they become part of our Low German also. We don't notice when we are in the States. Only when we return to Germany or have German visitors does someone point out that our speech has been invaded.

Nanne and his family live on a farm. He is a well-to-do farmer. He has cows, pigs, and an impressive amount of land around him. There are no comforting neighborhood houses close by; the nearest town is five miles away. We can't walk there, and bicycles are unknown here. We are stuck.

But I get to explore the land. I find a small creek, scare myself to death at the first real live snake I have ever seen, and explore. I don't work, even though Nanne's family thinks a young boy of nine should do something. We wait for several weeks while our temporary home in another town is being prepared. My parents are anxious to leave and be in their own house.

But their first place is a disaster. Three tiny rooms, an outhouse behind the house, and a dirt basement. My mother cried as she looked at it, and remembered her nice three-year-old brick house in Germany. This was not progress. Yet she pulled herself together, started cleaning with a vengeance, and planted the huge garden full of potatoes. Like the Irish, Germans see potatoes as their lifeblood.

It's late April. I have to go to school, as does my sister. We live in Shell Rock, a small town in Butler County. The school is across the river, and we walk there every day.

Of course, I can't speak any English. To help me learn, it is decided to place me in first grade instead of third grade where I belong. After all, learning English must be easier in first grade.

I learn very little. Math is easy, except when students mistake my German ones for sevens. I know better, and eventually the teacher figures it out. I'm periodically quizzed by a teacher who thinks she speaks German. It's Greek to me.

But I survive. In the summer I get to hang around the baseball field, and even get to go on bus trips with the team. I have no idea what I have to do, but I tag along. By the end of the summer I can speak enough English to translate for my parents.

The Statue of Liberty does promise a land of opportunity. In Germany, Amerika is considered a land where everyone grows rich. Money falls from trees. My father, in later years, often remarked that this turned out to be true. But, he always added, no one understood how hard one had to shake that tree. In Shell Rock, in the summer and fall of 1956, the money tree was nonexistent. It would not bear fruit for the next ten years.

Farm Life

In our part of Germany, immigrants who leave always farm. The promise of land to people who struggle on a few acres is a powerful lure. Land means wealth, land is opportunity. I suspect this was, in part, what drove my parents to leave Ostfriesland.

But the roaming instinct had to be present before that. My great-grandfather, Wilhelm Schoon, left Germany, a wife, and three children after World War I to come to Iowa. The official story is that he left to find a better place.

The unofficial story, and one denied by my elderly relatives, is infinitely more alluring. It holds that he went to the county fair, got drunk, engaged a gypsy in a knife-fight, and thought he had killed him. Fearing the authorities, he went home, gathered a few belongings, collected what cash there was from among the relatives, and slipped across the border to Amsterdam. There he caught a ship and found his way to Iowa, where his wife had relatives.

The happy ending, from the gypsy's perspective, was that he was not killed. Supposedly only his ear was cut off, and my grandfather need not have fled. Whether true or not—and I leave that to my daughter to discover—he did take off. He also left a delicious story to tell our children and grandchildren.

My father must also have been a roamer. When he was thirteen, his mother died in the German depression. His family had no money, his father quickly remarried to have someone to take care of the children, and he also left. He became a cook on a ship, and then traveled around the world for years. I do not know where he all went, and wish I had quizzed him more carefully. But that roaming must have been in his blood. To take his family and leave for a foreign country takes more courage than I would have.

But the heritage has been passed on. Both my daughters have the spirit. Both have traveled extensively and freely throughout the world as they grew into adulthood. I suspect genetics plays a part.

While the traveling spirit passed on, the lust for land was not genetic. My father was not a farmer. When we finally managed to start living on my great-grandfather's farm a few miles out of Waverly, it was not in a luxurious home.

The house was old and shabby, with a rickety old porch. The yard was full of nails, which, over time, my mother raked and cleaned as she cleaned everything else. But it was home, and would remain so for the next eight years.

The land was something else. It was a hundred acre farm, which, in those days, was enough to sustain a frugal farm family. But that assumes one had cows, pigs, machinery, and, most of all, credit. We had nothing.

The farm had been in my great-grandfather's name. When he and his wife become too old to farm, it was rented out. They lived in town. When he died, my grandmother went back to Germany. The land stayed, but it took time to change the title over to my parents. Fortunately, one lawyer in Germany and one in Shell Rock helped. After two years, it finally passed to my parents. They could borrow money to farm.

Before that, we got by. Older Germans who were more established helped. They donated time, a cow or two, came to butcher pigs, castrate the little pigs, and show my dad what to buy in machinery. We gradually accumulated cows, pigs, and chickens.

Cows were the lifeblood. They provided the only regular cash income to the family. We acquired them one by one as we could afford them. Most were named, frequently after the family that had sold them to us.

My job was to get the cows from the pasture, drive them into the barn, and sometimes feed them. One has to do that slowly, since cows ready to be milked don't like to be pushed. But to a ten-year-old eager to return to his book, making them move faster was more exciting.

But one had to be careful! One old cow, "Winkey," would not be pushed. She would turn on you, find you irritating, and try to butt you. She'd butt you again if you tried to pass in front of her when feeding the other cows.

I also had to avoid pushing cows when I got close to the barn. My father would see that, and would yell. Cows let milk go early if pushed too hard, and that's money wasted.

But cows were at least interesting. Chickens were awful. They stayed in an old chicken house, and my job was to feed them, and sometimes to gather the eggs. Hens sitting on nests do not like to be disturbed, and their pecks on young hands are painful. Also, even though feeding them took only a short time, there were far more interesting things to do. Yet, for some reason, parents do not understand that. In their view, chickens must be fed, and must be fed every night. So I do not remember chickens with fondness.

The land eventually produced more products. We raised corn, beans, and hay. The corn was the most profitable. Corn, and I mean the American maize, grows in ears, on a cob. It is the bread of Iowa farm life. We grow it, we try to harvest as much of it as we can, and we continually increase the levels of production. In 2002, on my farm fields, it is common to harvest 150 to 170 bushels for every acre.

In 1956, we were lucky to harvest forty to fifty bushels per acre. We did not have the hybrid seed we now have, we did not have the ability to plant a large number of plants per acre, and we did not have the ability to harvest hundreds of acres. A 100-acre farm might support a family, and a farmer who had paid off all the debt on a 160-acre farm—or, God forbid, 240 acres—was rich. But with cows, pigs, chickens, and sometimes geese, we survived.

We rarely sold corn back then. Corn was grown to feed the hogs and cows. Especially the hogs. They grew fat on it and were then sold or butchered.

We also used it to heat our house. When we first came to the farm, we had a wood-burning stove and eventually a furnace. A furnace heats the whole house with heating ducts. A stove sits on the main floor of the house and heats only a small area around it. The bedrooms get little heat; the upstairs none. We had a circular hole in the living room ceiling, which allowed heat to rise from the stove below it into the room where Willie and I slept. There was no other heat. When it was twenty below we seldom lingered in that room. The single pane windows would be a solid sheet of ice. But my mother had brought her featherbeds from Germany and we were warm as long as we stayed under them.

The heating hole served another unintended purpose. We could listen to everything that was said downstairs, assuming it was not too cold to stick our heads out of the covers. This often produced valuable tidbits of information that we were not supposed to know.

Unfortunately it worked both ways. The hole also allowed our parents to listen to us. By standing below it they could hear when we got into fights or arguments; I recall many a threat coming from below, describing our terrible fates if we did not quiet down and go to sleep.

Meta had it worse. Her small room adjoined ours, but it did not have a heating hole. Thus I think she was often even colder than we were. Worse yet, she had to come through our room to get to hers. Navigating through the bedroom of two squabbling brothers was probably not her idea of fun.

But Meta was a girl, and as such had some advantages. She didn't have to help with the corn cobs, for example.

Corn cobs burn easily. They don't burn long, nor give off much heat, but they do burn quite well. And, most important of all, they were free. So we used our corn cobs to heat our house.

This meant loading them on a wagon, driving the wagon to the house, opening the cellar storm door, and shoveling the corn cobs down the stairs. From there they had to be piled against the wall, where they could be shoveled into the furnace. I was often drafted to help with those chores. My father would be in the basement and my mother and I would be on top, pushing the cobs from the wagon down the stairs.

We progressed from the initial stove to the cob-burning furnace, and, luxury at last, to an oil-fired furnace. But the latter took years to arrive. By then I was gone. But I still remember the first furnace, the wood I helped to saw, and the corn cobs that kept us warm those first cold winters.

Corn cobs have other uses to inventive children. One can stab a chicken feather or two in one end and throw them like arrows. They fly quite straight. It is then easier to hit your brother with them. To prevent injury, and to imitate knights in shining armor, one can borrow pot lids from one's mother's kitchen and pretend they are shields. In this manner corn cob missiles can be deflected.

But sometimes the game got too rough. I was twelve and Willie was six. I was faster and could throw better. Our games would typically end with me hitting him on his head and then his inevitable crying. As the older and more responsible party, the blame for that was always mine. After all, my parents would point out, I could hit him in the eye, and then where would we be. They were right. But it was fun, and I could usually talk him into doing it again.

We lived from the corn we produced. We fed it to our animals, then ate their meat and drank their milk. We stayed warm from the leftover cobs, and finally exercised our minds by using them to invent new means of torturing our siblings. It was a very useful plant.

But growing corn was not easy. In the spring, one had to plow the ground, then disc it, then rake it, and then plant it. After planting, the cultivator was put on the tractor, and there were several trips across the fields to clean out the weeds. Straight rows of corn are important, as are straight furrows. Corn planted in rectangular patterns must have straight rows. Curvy or wavy lines of corn are a sign of a poor farmer. The best farmers would only have arrow straight rows of corn. It was a common pastime to drive around through the country roads on Sunday afternoon to look at the growing fields, and see which farmers had clean fields, and straight rows. Old habits die hard. I still do it today some fifty years later.

In the old days, to plant corn, the ground had to be prepared. As it has been done for thousands of years, a plow is used to turn over the ground. The remaining corn stalks from prior years are buried into the ground where they will decompose and add nutrients back to the soil.

But plowing leaves a very rough surface, unsuitable for planting. To even out the surface, discing is next. A disc is composed of several rows of metal disks that cut into the ground and slice any remaining residue. Instead of slicing straight into the ground, this row of rolling discs is set at an angle, so the dirt is disturbed. The heavy furrows are evened out, and the ground is closer to being ready.

But there was another step to prepare the ground, raking. A rake is like a metal mattress with iron teeth sticking into the ground. As it is dragged across the surface, the clods of dirt are torn apart even more, and the field becomes even. Now it ready for the corn planter.

Corn in the old days was planted one kernel at a time, about a foot apart. The growing corn would look like a checkerboard, with corn growing on each corner.

The rows must be even from both directions to allow cultivation. Weeds do not respect such order and grow everywhere in such fertile soil. To ensure even distribution and straight rows, wires were laid across the fields. The wires fed into the planter and contained knots at regular one foot intervals. As each knot pulled through the planter, a disc turned, and one kernel of corn dropped into the ground. At the end of the row the tractor and planter were turned around, the wire was moved, and another two rows of corn were planted. Equal spacing was important.

Cultivating came next to control the weeds. A cultivator is like a hoe, but mounted on or pulled behind a tractor. The tractor would be driven through the rows of corn, the tines carefully set to disturb only the ground between the rows. Then, when the corn had been cultivated in one direction, it had to be cultivated from the sides. Thus, only the corn plants were left on this checkerboard.

But even that was not enough. The tines of cultivators could not be set too close to the corn plants, and some weeds grew close to the plant. If portions of the field were heavily infested, we would have to hoe the remaining weeds by hand.

Morning glories were the worst weed. They grew close to the corn stalk and infested patches of fields. Weeding them was a job for ten-year-olds, and one not appreciated by this ten-year-old. Fortunately, most fields were fairly clean, and we seldom had to hoe much by hand.

At harvest, corn had to be combined. A combine was pulled behind the tractor, and the ears were stored in open bins to be fed to pigs. My harvesting job was to drive the tractor to open the fields. Corn was planted fence row to fence row, and the tractor and combine needed at least six open rows to function. Therefore, the first six rows around a field had to be picked by hand.

I would come home from school, quickly change into last year's jeans (no good school clothes while working) and slowly drive the tractor while my parents picked the corn by hand. It took several weeks before the combine could be used. Some farmers drove over those corn rows and wasted those rows. That would have been an anathema to good German sensibilities.

In our more modern times, we no longer plant corn in such a manner. We may disc the land in the fall or spring, and the newer planters are strong enough to cut through the residue. Also, instead of a two-row planter, we have eight- or sixteen-row planters. We also do not cultivate. One pass of herbicides takes care of the weeds, and nothing more is done. The plow is forgotten and no longer used. Huge combines harvest six, eight, or ten rows at a pass. The ear is stripped from the plant, shelled immediately, and the cob is shredded and dumped back on the field. The hopper fills rapidly with yellow gold and the combine rarely stops as it is augured into a wagon, carefully driven parallel to the air-conditioned combine, equipped with AM/FM radio and a CD player. When the field is done, the farmer can have the combine's computer print out a pretty colored map of the fields, with different colors representing the yield for every row. Based on that map, the farmer can tell where the field was wet, where more fertilizer may be needed, or which particular hybrid did best.

In the old days (my young days), we had only a wagon, a tractor, and a pull-behind corn picker. The tractor pulled the picker, the wagon was hitched to the picker, and the yellow ear corn was fed into the wagon. When the wagon was full, it was unhitched, replaced, and the full wagon hauled back to the farm. The ear corn then went into slatted buildings, or corn cribs, to dry. The sides were sufficiently ventilated to allow the movement of air, and the ear corn was sufficiently rough to allow air to flow naturally through the crib. It dried by itself.

Now, on my farm, I have two small grain bins holding 10,000 bushels of shelled corn. "Small" is the operative word. A 50,000 bushel bin is more common. Each bin has a huge electrical fan on it, and the fan must be turned on to push sufficient moisture through the grain to dry the corn. Corn must have a moisture content of no more than fifteen to sixteen percent, or it will rot. Fourteen is ideal. Twelve is too low, and elevators add water to keep the weight up.

But in our time we had no idea what the moisture content of our corn might be. If it was yellow and hard it was harvested and placed in the cribs. There it stayed until the pigs got hungry. One would fill a bushel basket, or pail, with ear corn, carry it by hand to the pig pen, and dump it on the ground—or, if one was more modern, on concrete. Concrete wasted less corn. The pigs then ate the yellow corn and left the cobs.

Later, as we became more advanced, the ear corn could be shelled. Shelling meant an enormous truck would come to the farm, set up next to the corn crib, and the ear corn would be shoveled into the machine. It would separate the corn from the cob. The shelled corn could then be sold, or, more frequently, ground into feed with other additives and fed as a supplement to the cows.

The cobs were another matter. They were heaped in big piles. Sometimes they might be ground and mixed with feed, or they could be loaded on a wagon and hauled back into the field. They would decompose and the cycle would start again.

Soybeans are similar. But soybeans have their own problems. Usually planted where corn was planted the year before, a soybean field always has volunteer corn that can't be uprooted by a cultivator or herbicides. Thus, one has to "walk beans." With a hoe in hand, one walks the long rows, hacking out the volunteers that want to compete with the beans. This is hard work for a young child. It is boring, it is hot, and the beans are often wet, as is the ground.

But one must walk the beans. Having dirty bean fields is a disgrace among the neighbors. One can always tell a lazy neighbor by his bean field. If there is corn in it, that is a sin. Obviously such a person has no pride, and is condemned by the Sunday drivers.

That tradition continued. I remember my parents returning from their traumatic escape to Germany after my brother was killed and buying another farm to have something to do. They again planted corn and beans, or had someone plant it for them. But beans must be walked and pride must be served, even though my parents no longer needed the money as badly. At the age of sixty, my mother would insist my dad arise at 5 a.m. and go walk the beans in the early morning hours before it got too hot. My dad would later confide to me that he finally gave up farming and rented out the ground because he was tired of this.

Making hay on a farm was also hard work, with many stresses over the weather.

Haymaking in Amerika is different than making hay in Germany. Back in Ostfriesland, my grandfather, Opa Walle, had a small farm, a horse, pigs, and a number of cows. Cows need hay in the winter. Opa's land around his barn was quite small, and was used to grow rye, potatoes, and pasture for the cows. But he had some land about fifteen miles away, called "Meeden." This was land in a flat, sour area, where regular crops could not be grown. Formerly, some 500 or 600 years ago, it might have been under the North Sea, or at least subject to periodic flooding. But by the 1950s it was protected by an extensive system of dikes around Ostfriesland.

The only thing this land produced was one crop of long, stringy grass hay. It had to be cut, dried, and hauled back to Walle. But in Ostfriesland it rains a lot. If hay is left on the ground and it rains, it doesn't dry very well, and can rot. So in the olden days, when everything was done by hand, the hay would often be placed on wooden racks. It would be off the ground and dry much faster, but avoid rotting if it rained.

My father, sensing a business opportunity, started selling those wooden racks to farmers. He would go out after work in the summer and pedal his bike for twenty or thirty miles, talking to farmers. He was always good at talking, and, from his surveying days, would often know which farmer was in the market for such wood. He made a few extra marks being the middleman. Now, when I go back to Germany, I periodically drive by car the roads he pedaled and wonder at the energy it took. (But bicycling came naturally to my parents. They thought nothing of a ten or twenty mile trip. Even in their retirement years they would pedal their bicycles to Walle, a distance of ten miles, pedal back for lunch at home, and back again for afternoon festivities. In fact, when I was forty, I rode with him once. I was soon out of breath, and he, at seventy-eight, looked at me and asked, "You're not in very good shape, are you?" He had trouble maintaining his balance while walking, or getting on and off the bike, but, by God, once going, he could go forever.)

But back to Opa Walle. Once the hay was cut, and dried sufficiently to haul back home, everyone would go to the field and fork the hay on the wagon. The horse would slowly walk through the field and Opa and any helpers would toss the loose hay on the wagon. Usually they took two wagons. When one was filled, the other would then be loaded. Then the two wagons would be hitched together, and the horse would have to haul them back to Walle.

We, as kids, got to tag along sometimes. I was too little to do much work, but could play, try to catch frogs in the ditches, and otherwise get in the way. At the end of the long day I would climb on top of the wagon full of hay and fall asleep as we slowly went back to Walle.

My mother remembers doing the same thing when she was small. But she also remembers the poor times. The wagon had to go through Moordorf, a village full of really poor people. Moordorf was the Poland of our area. Kaiser Wilhelm, in the late 1890s, gave soldiers land rights, and some came to Moordorf. Then, it was truly a moor. The area was covered with peat moors, which had to be dug out by hand. It was a miserable existence. That memory lingered. My mother is a bit ashamed to come from such a place, but she was born there. Even now, she is reluctant to admit that is the place of her birth.

In the late 1920s or l930s, poverty still reigned in Moordorf. People who lived there kept rabbits for extra food, and rabbits also had to eat in hard times. As the hay wagon went through the village street, children would try to pull out loose hay from the wagons to feed their rabbits. Opa Walle would try to protect his hay, and would, on occasion, lash out with his horse whip to keep the children away from the wagons. My mother remembers that with shame. But at the time Opa Walle needed the hay for his cows and his family, so he no doubt felt he had no choice.

But in my young years those times were past. No pesky children bothered us as we trundled back home. I always wonder how the poor horse pulled two heaping loads of hay, but he did. I often fell asleep in the fragrant hay, and did not awake until we arrived back in Walle. I was then trundled off to bed.

The work did not stop there. The wagons had to be placed in the barn and unloaded. The loose hay was tossed into the haymow and piled high for the winter. It would stay there until it was used. But storing hay was not quite that easy. The hay must be dry. If it got too wet it would increase in heat and could spontaneously burst into flames. There are many stories of farmers getting too anxious, storing wet hay, and having it burst into flames. Then the whole house and barn go up in smoke. All is lost.

Opa Walle watched his stored hay carefully. He had a long iron rod, which he would drive into the hay, and it would heat up. When he withdrew it, he could tell from the warmth of the rod whether the hay might ignite. In his barn, it never did. I often wonder if his first house, which did burn up, taught him to be careful. I guess I'll never know the answer to that question.

Haying in Iowa was different. Here, we had alfalfa hay, not grass hay. Alfalfa is a grass. The seed is mixed with oat seed and sprayed on the field in late March. The earlier the seeding, the better. Oats germinate quickly and grow very fast. It can be harvested in July. But the alfalfa seed mixed with the oat seed grows much slower. It does establish a base, and, once the oats are harvested, the alfalfa takes over. It will then grow in the now-empty field, and, the next year, will be ready for harvest.

Alfalfa has a much higher nutritional value to cows than grass hay. Agronomists can tell you how much, but I cannot. Suffice it to say alfalfa feeds more cows for longer than grass hay does. Alfalfa can also be harvested more than once. Once established, it grows fast. A first cutting can be made in June, a second in late July, and, sometimes, a third cutting in late September. But the first cutting is by far the best.

In early June, the alfalfa is growing rapidly. It is at least a foot high. A tractor and a mechanical mower are used to cut the alfalfa. A sickle mower chops down the fragrant rows, and the rows lay on the ground to dry. In Amerika we don't need the wooden racks to facilitate drying. The hay dries in two or three days and then it's ready for baling. Sometimes, in later years, a conditioner, which is nothing but a press that squeezes the hay as it is cut, is pulled behind the mower. The hay is squeezed, the moisture is driven out, and it dries more quickly.

To encourage drying, a windrower is used to flip the rows of cut hay. This turns over the hay and reduces the chance of rot. Once dry, a baler arrives. A baler sucks in the rows of hay, a ram tightly packs the hay into bales, the bales are wrapped in twine, and pushed out the back end of the baler. A flat bed wagon is hitched behind the baler, and a young energetic man, stationed on the flat bed, grabs the finished bales and stacks them on the wagon. Once the wagon is full, another wagon is prepared and the process starts all over.

The loaded wagon is then hauled to the barn. There, it is placed under the haymow and a mechanical "jaw" is dropped from the top of the barn. Jaws are pushed into the hay bales, the load of hay is raised into the air, into the barn, a rope is pulled, the hay bales are dropped, and the jaws return for a new load.

People are needed for all these tasks. Someone must drive the tractor that pulls the baler. Someone must be on the flat bed wagon loading the bales. Someone has to drive the full load of hay back to the barn. (Remember, the tractor and baler don't stop—time and weather are precious, and getting the hay off the ground is the most critical part of the operation) Then, someone has to stick the jaws into the hay, someone has to drive the tractor that provides the force that pulls the hay into the air and into the barn, and someone has to be inside the haymow to stack the bales that drop from the jaws. Haying takes lots of people, and lots of luck.

My job, at age ten or eleven or twelve, was as a driver. I was not trusted to drive the tractor that pulled the baler. I was too small to load the bales of hay on the flat bed. But I could drive the tractor to and from the fields, and I could drive the tractor that provided the energy to pull the loads of hay into the barn. So I was drafted. My father usually drove the tractor in the field, or stacked the bales of hay on the flat bed.

My mother did not drive tractors. She was usually elected to push the jaws into the hay bales, and release them when they had reached the correct distance. She was also responsible for food. This was important. We worked all day, but always took time out for food. A big breakfast, morning tea and snacks, a huge lunch, and an afternoon tea break were mandatory. My mother somehow provided all that, in large quantities, and we never felt hungry. Then, when all that was done, she and my father still had to milk the cows.

I remember haying time as a fun time, but a tense time. The weather might not cooperate. Rains came and went; the weather forecast on the radio was critical, and the availability of help was essential. We couldn't do it alone. I still remember Fritz and Lini, our German friends from Davenport—who helped us many a time, and who were not farmers—with grateful thanks. Fritz was big and strong, and Lini was of the old German school in her approach to cooking. Without their help, we might not have survived it.

Haying time was tough. But it also was fun. It taught me the value of cooperation, of work, and of friends who cared. I can only hope I have helped others like the friends who helped us in those early days.

Our land in Amerika was not the best. About thirty to forty acres would flood periodically, and thus could rarely be planted. Only in especially dry springs could a crop be planted in this low spot.

Fortunately for my parents, the United States had too much grain. Some land was set aside, and the government paid farmers for setting aside good farmland. Our wetlands qualified in those more benign days, and, as a result, sometimes produced more cash than the land we laboriously farmed. Fifty years later, that has not changed.

But in my young mind, I did not think of land as something that produced wealth. It simply existed, and it produced work. We never left the farm, except for infrequent trips to friends or to town, and I soon longed to escape it. Yet, without realizing it at the time, the lure of land, and the love of land, had become ingrained. That farm is still there today. I returned to live in the country, on my own land, and have no desire to leave it for good. Somehow, without realizing how it came to be, the same desire of my forefathers still possesses me today.

Johann and Hilda Fokkena, summer 1984, in Oldenburg, Germany.

Johann was born in Georgsheil, another village outside Aurich in Ostfriesland. His mother died when he was young, and his father quickly remarried. He and his siblings were not close to their stepmother and left home early. Johann couldn't afford to stay in school, so he got a job as a cook on a private ship and later joined the Arbeitsdienst, which subsequently became part of the army. After World War II he became a land surveyor and then moved to the U.S. in 1956, where he farmed until his retirement.

The pin Hilda is wearing in this photograph is inscribed with the names and birthdates of her five grandchildren.

"It Was a Wild Time in American Culture and We Enjoyed It"

By Mike Heffner

I met Willie Fokkena in the fall of 1969 when he came from Iowa to spend the school year with his sister who lived in my hometown of Williamsport, Pennsylvania. Williamsport had a population of about 40,000 and our high school had about 2,500 students at that time due to the "baby boomer" generation, of which we were a part. My earliest recollection of Willie was reading an article in our school newspaper about the foreign exchange students who would be attending our school. Willie was erroneously listed as an exchange student from Germany. He was in a few of my classes so I introduced myself and we immediately struck up a friendship.

Willie was very cool and calm and a keen observer, a little shy but very bright and funny. I liked him right away and it turned out we had a lot in common. We were enrolled in the academic course of study and shared chemistry and phys. ed. class. We were not really interested in school at that point in our lives. Although our country and culture were going through great changes and it was the beginning of a very liberal and free era, you would not have known it by attending our school. Classes were very boring and there was no attempt to introduce any excitement or liveliness into the classroom. It was intellectually numbing to a creative person like Willie to sit through the long boring days. We just did not take it seriously and did not do very well. I remember seeing him writing in a spiral bound notebook all the time. It turned out he was writing poems, which he showed me. I thought that was pretty cool and started writing some, too. We would write poems in each other's notebooks and I still have a few that he wrote in mine.

I found as I got to know Willie that he was interested in a wide variety of things, especially in writing, art, music, and philosophy. I remember him carrying a little book of Zen essays around with him and that really knocked me out. We felt that we could learn more on our own than we could in school. We spent a lot of time at the public library looking for books that were more interesting to us than what we were learning in school. We were kind of "anti-establishment," which was cool at that time. We were not actively protesting or rebelling against anything, just going off in our own direction. It was a wild time in American culture and we enjoyed it.

Willie liked sports and played on the basketball team for a while and was in the German Club for a time also. He was tall and thin with fine blond hair and was quite striking in appearance. The girls found him to be attractive and he had a girlfriend named Linda that he was close to in the spring of 1970. For the most part we mocked and made fun of our stuffy, boring teachers. I can still see Willie impersonating our phys. ed. teacher Mr. Myers, who reminded us both of W.C. Fields. He would say, *"Listen to Mr. Myers—he knows"* in the same Fieldsian way that our teacher did and it would crack me up. I recently opened up my 1970 yearbook to see what Willie had written and, sure enough, there in his unmistakable handwriting is written, *"Listen to Mr. Myers. He knows."*

We were driven to the verge of craziness by our chemistry teacher, Mr. Salvatori. Class was tedious and dreary and our only relief came when we would go to the lab. There we would work together as a team doing unfathomable experiments. I recall Willie heating up some kind of glassware, a beaker or something, over a flame and asking Mr. Salvatori a question, probably as a joke rather than out of any real desire to understand the class. Mr. Salvatori, unaware that the beaker was hot, came over and took it from Willie, burning his hand and dropping the beaker, shattering it on the floor. Willie just looked at me with a quizzical look on his face as if to ask "what are we doing here?"

We were caught up in the music and style of the time. We wore bellbottoms and both loved The Beatles; *Abbey Road* was our favorite album. Occasionally we would go to hear bands at a little place only a few blocks from Willie's house. There was some amazing music during those days and we loved it. Our country was going through some big changes at that time but we were just seventeen-year-old kids enjoying ourselves and the freedom that was ours. I don't recall that we were too involved or interested in the politics of the day. We were against the war in Vietnam and I can't imagine either of us going to fight. I think Willie was a pacifist at heart. We were observers of the events of those days, not participants. We were interested but we were more likely to discuss what we were planning for the weekend. Could we find someone to buy us beer and then maybe hear a band play somewhere? I can tell you that there was a great sense of freedom that we felt in 1969-1970. There were not as many rules and regulations; it was a much looser, freer time. There were no computers, cell phones, internet, VCRs, MTV, AIDS, etc. etc. It was a good time to come of age and Willie was the perfect person to share it with.

I was aware that Willie was from a German family. That is what first attracted me to him. I was and still am always happy to meet someone from another country or culture and maybe learn something new. Willie helped me with my German and was probably the main reason I passed German that year. I am of German heritage too, so I was especially glad to know him, but we never really discussed that aspect of his life. I knew he had strong ties to Germany and thought how great it would be to visit Germany someday, but we were young and concerned with what was right in front of us each day. We had no concern for the future at that point. We were on a wild ride and the future would take care of itself.

Recently I got out a letter Willie wrote to me and reread it. He talks about working for his Dad for $5 a day but going to check with another farmer and maybe making $60 a week. He mentions buying "Let It Be" for $6 and states that "it is the best Beatles album yet." He says that he is teaching himself to play piano. He talks about his brother wrecking his 350 Yamaha. He tells about going to a celebration in town called "Pioneer Days" and closes by telling me to bring my golf clubs when I come out, as his family had joined a club where we could swim and play golf. (He knew I didn't have golf clubs and didn't play golf.)

It's been thirty-two years since I've spoken to him and I still miss him. I always had the feeling that Willie was very bright and capable and would put his considerable talent to work when he was ready. I have often wondered what he would have done had he survived. I think he could have been an artist, writer, actor, filmmaker, philosopher, professor. Who knows? I am certain that he would have been successful at anything he chose to do. I have thought about him for thirty-two years and I am pleased to be in contact with his family and share my memories of him. It is so strange that this is coming about after all this time; it seems there is some crazy cosmic mystery at play here. It is wonderful watching it reveal itself. I almost feel like Willie is watching this and getting a big kick out of it.

Spring

By Willie Fokkena

I opened the door in the morning
And instinctively flinched to meet the cold,
But the wind whispered gently across my face
And for the rest of the day I saw spring unfold.
And the morning didn't seem so bad.

I walked down the sidewalk
Now free from the clutches of snow,
And the ground it was soft
And the sky it was blue
And the sun shone its magic on all.

A mockingbird perched in the tree
That had stood lonely and brave that winter
Among the litter and weeds of an empty lot,
But now it had a friend.
It already started to mend
From the ravages of winter.

And I saw the most fantastic breathtaking sight:
A small green blade of grass had poked through the mud
And in my mind I could see a field of green
And a fly, I saw a fly!
And I remembered how I had cursed that
Persistent little fiend ages ago.
I swore to myself, knowing I would break it
That I would never curse him again.

And people. I saw people! Their faces!
Each of us had passed each other many times before
Each lost in his own routine; heads bent to fight
The icy breath of that cold monster now defeated.
But now I saw their faces and they saw mine
And we smiled.
Everyone looked so beautiful.
It seemed that we had been living under the strict
Eyes of some overseer with a whip who
Would snap us if we looked up or smiled.

The mystical calvary had come to the rescue
And had driven him away with fire
And rescued our souls, that were slipping into the
Unreturnable depths of isolation just in time.
We smiled and said "Hello."

And I felt that I could defeat anything
And I had to run, like a young colt,
Confined in a ten by fifteen box all his life.
Then for the first time he sees the full extent
Of the world he was born in but didn't know.
He kicks his heels and uncertainly canters
Over soft, rich smelling, strands of green carpet,
But reassured by his mother's beckening glance
Races behind her out into the universe
And life starts anew.

Ray and Meta Brost, outside their home in Oldenburg, Germany, summer 1991. After their three children finished high school they retired and moved back to the U.S.

My brother Garrelt and I lived in Walle with our grandparents, Habbe and Gertje Lueken. Meta lived close by and would walk over to see us. We had to do chores but she always managed to lure us out to play. She knew just how to persuade Oma to let us go. Meta and Garrelt were best friends; they always stuck together. Most of the time Meta was a peacemaker but sometimes her temper would get the best of her. I remember a time we pulled each other's hair and she won! When Meta got older, about fourteen, she spent more time with me; she needed a girl cousin. She was fifteen when she, together with her entire family, left Walle and emigrated to the USA. We did not see each other again until 1963 when she met me at the airport on the day I, too, immigrated. It was extremely nice of her to be there!

~Gerda Taylor

The Steam Whistle As Fire Alarm

By Ray Brost

Sixty years ago, when I was a boy, the only fire alarms and emergency vehicle warnings you heard were those that wail up and down—like in old Mack Sennett films. Nowadays fire alarms and emergency vehicles all have extra noise-makers: woop-woop-woop, braak-braak-braak, dee-dah-dee-dah-dee-dah, and so forth. Could it be that my father, Henry Brost (1899–1963), is to blame for this change?

It happened when he was Fire Chief of the Medford, WI Volunteer Fire Department that some firemen living in the southwest end of town missed out on an occasional winter night's run because they had not been awakened by the fire siren up on the old, centrally-located water tower. Medford had become too spread out.

So my dad refurbished a steam whistle from one of the old sawmills he had salvaged in the late 1930s and then he talked the city fathers into having it mounted atop the Medford Cooperative Creamery. The creamery was ideal for this because it was located in the southwest part of town, was manned day and night, and always maintained a head of steam.

A short article in the *Star News* alerted the populace, but the first combined use of the siren and whistle startled everyone anyway. Accompanying the steady up and down of the penetrating and nerve-rasping siren on the water tower came this comical mix of horrible screeches, toots, bellows and squeaks. Someone was pulling on the whistle cord to vary the sound, all right, but the pitch change could not be controlled and it would jump unpredictably from one weird resonance to another.

So the thing had to be dismounted and reworked, and it was in my dad's shop again, getting adjusted, polished and tweaked—a brassy metal thing, clearly the love child of a teakettle and an artillery shell. Then, back on top of the creamery it sounded just the same: not exactly The Ode To Joy.

But the city fathers decided it would just have to do. Now the creamery employees had a merry time of making that whistle blow; every fire was a chance to experiment, and it was blown differently depending on who was on duty. Some did a mix that showed a talent for jazz; others tried to make it go up and down with the water tower siren, which had the effect of Jerry Lewis trying to impersonate Tina Turner. Eventually some of the workers got quite good at holding it at pretty much the same pitch for a few seconds.

And the people of Medford, being confident of the ways of the Lord, accepted it, and it became part of the culture of the town, sparing only the deaf in the wee hours of those bitter-cold nights when chimney fires were so frequent. Then, when your deep slumber was infiltrated by those eerie steam whistle notes you felt a kind of chill in your soul that no modern alarm system, however cleverly designed, could ever induce.

Letters From Germany

By Clara (Fokkena) Hinman

Nov. 8, 1998

Dear Laura and Lisa,

In keeping with the tone of the following letters, I will describe what is happening now. I'm here with Rakaya. She is four years old. She has a Monopoly game out and is trying to figure out what it is all about.

It snowed during the night, and we had fun walking through the wet snow to the school where we had breakfast provided by the local fire fighters at their fundraiser.

As I read through the letters, the events are still so clear in my mind I can't believe thirty years have gone by. At the end of one of the Laura Ingalls Wilder books she says, "Now is now and can never be a long time ago." I still live in that state of denial myself.

Sometimes the letters trigger more memories. I will add the thoughts I think you might find meaningful.

The letters start June 16, 1968. Habbo and I were married April 6, 1968, two days after Martin Luther King, Jr. was assassinated. Habbo left for Germany two weeks later after his advanced infantry training at Fort Gordon, Georgia. This was during the Vietnam era, and we were thrilled to be stationed in Europe. Soon after Habbo arrived in Germany, he was able to return to Walle and Georgshiel where he visited his relatives. He hadn't seen most of them since his family left Germany in 1956. His grandfather, your Opa's father, told him he was going to die, but he would wait to meet me.

I was student teaching at the Price Lab School at UNI in Cedar Falls. I graduated May 31, 1968 and left for Germany two weeks later, which happened to be a few days after Robert Kennedy was shot in California.

In 1968 Grandma Ellie was 43, Grandpa was 53, and Ann was 3. I was 23, and Habbo was 21. Grandma Ellie kept the letters in a safe place all these years and occasionally reminded me of their existence.

Somehow 1998 seems like a fitting time to be arranging for each of you to have a copy of the letters. I can't believe I didn't know you as I was writing the original letters!

Love,
Mom

June 16, 1968

Dear Mama, Daddy, and Ann,

Well, here we are in Germany! I'll start with right now and go back from there. The couple we are staying with is unbelievably nice. They have made things very convenient for us. The room is just the right size, and we can watch TV with them and put food for snacks in their refrigerator, but until they leave, we eat out. We just returned from having supper outside by a lake in a big old beautiful park. The town is Bad Neuheim. It is known as a health resort like Glenwood Springs, Colorado.

The flight was fun and everything was fine. On the German plane I sat between a 65-year-old lady going to Yugoslavia for three weeks and a Greek man going to Athens. Both of them made the flight more interesting and fun. We flew over London and Belgium, but because of clouds below we didn't see anything.

Until we got into Frankfurt things looked much like Iowa, but in Frankfurt everything turned German. The buildings are very old and there are flower gardens everywhere. Germany doesn't have mosquitoes so it is fun to eat outside. Even on the lake where it was humid and warm, insects didn't bother us. We had a very simple German meal, but it was good. Today is the first day of summer for them (well, that's what I was told) and some of the German girls are wearing native German costumes just as they go about their regular business. They dress that way today and tomorrow.

From what I can tell, my simple A-line dresses are just fine. I had heard so much about how they dress up that I thought perhaps everyone wore suits or something. They simply wear dresses rather than running around in shorts or with curlers in their hair. So far everything I had been apprehensive about has turned out to be better than I expected.

Habbo met me with six long-stemmed red roses for graduation. They are setting here in a vase on the desk. They're beautiful. Habbo is reading; it's 9 o'clock p.m. and 2 o'clock p.m. for you. There are many big apartment houses in the American housing section. They are kind of plain looking on the outside, but the apartments are very nice. The German apartments have little balconies; their apartment houses are near here.

Your picture is by the roses, and so is the clock. It all looks very nice.

We're going to watch some German TV before we go to bed. We'll do several things tomorrow to get me going on my own so I don't have to be led around by the hand. The job situation looks hopeful. I'll be glad to have one, but I probably won't start until after Habbo's leave in July. There is plenty to keep me busy, however.

I hope you had a nice weekend and write soon.

June 18, 1968

It is Tuesday about 1:00 p.m. The only way I can begin to tell about everything is to write often. Yesterday we walked from Butzbach where Habbo works day and night (army clerk-typist in the daytime and bartender at the NCO Club at night) to our apartment. Our apartment is in a little area called "suburb in the woods." Actually the houses aren't in the woods, but you walk through the woods to get there. The area is very hilly, like foothills to mountains. This little village where our apartment is is almost at the top of the hill. Our kitchen faces the downward side and our little table sets under the window. You can look down on three or four villages or towns. We will live upstairs in the house and the people who own the house live downstairs. Each house has a tiny front yard and a bigger backyard. There are flowers and gardens all over. It's very picturesque. A house two or three houses from us has a little shallow, cement pond in front with goldfish in it.

[Note from 2002: In 1987 Habbo, Laura, the Shepard girls and I walked around in this neighborhood. Habbo didn't remember the goldfish pond and I couldn't find it. We asked a man standing on a balcony across the street. He remembered it, knew where it had been, and said it had been filled in!]

We'll have no hot water. In the bedroom is a little stove to heat by in the winter. They heat the downstairs, but said the little stove would be useful for us. There is a thigh-high refrigerator and a two-burner stove with a little oven. The freezer is about the size of a shoe box. From what I can tell, I brought just the right things. The people who own the house said they bought their set of dishes for $7.00. They were pretty, too.

I know I'll think of more, but I need to go and iron and get ready to take the bus to Butzbach (U.S. buses for dependents are free) and eat supper with Habbo. He works tonight. I'm going to get something for him to eat when he comes home at 1:00 a.m. I don't know what, but it seems like I should be up sometime. I was in bed when he left and don't want him to find me there when he comes home, too.

The army service club sponsors tours all the time and short ones on Sundays which we might take advantage of this Sunday. I wish I had my big purse. Write soon.

June 21, 1968

Guess what?!? I got a job!!!

Yesterday morning Audrey (the lady we're staying with—36, teacher, no children) and I went all over trying to find a job for me that would use my "ability as a teacher." We just kept getting long, complicated application forms which might not lead to anything. Anyway, I'd have to loaf until at least October when regular teachers start getting sick. The most hopeful prospect was working in a nursery perhaps until 1:00 a.m. It wouldn't have paid much. At noon Audrey left me in Butzbach to have lunch with Habbo. It started raining hard and I caught the train to Bad Nauheim and was sleeping here when Audrey came in from getting her hair fixed. She knocked on the door and said, "You've got a job if you want it."

She had talked to Ann, a lady upstairs who works in the book and magazine room at this PX. It's called the Stars and Stripes Bookstore and the lady who runs it at each town or base gets a commission. You set your own hours and the more you work, the more you make, of course. It is a good job, legitimate, and part of the army. They have a Stars and Stripes Bookstore wherever they have other facilities such as the snack bar, commissary, etc. The guys at Friedburg were complaining because the bookstore was always closed. She was also short about $200 and was asked to quit.

We both feel more settled and happier now that I have a niche. Oh, it will pay about $200 a month. Our apartment is $50 a month, so we ought to make ends meet. I'll get to sit down while I work and when no one is around, I can read and even eat my lunch to avoid closing at noon because that's when the guys want their papers and magazines.

If I'd known I was going to do this, I'd have bought my German dictionary and my recipe book from me! I bought them at the Stars and Stripes bookstore in Giessen.

One bad thing about it is you can't take a week off now and then to go on leaves. However, you can, and everyone does, close on all German and American holidays. Some Sunday in July, Ann, Gil, Jack, and Audrey are going to pick us up at 6:00 a.m. and take us with them on a boat trip on the Rhine. This area is right about in the middle so we can go either up or down the river. Most of the old castles are to the south, but there is much to see to the north also.

In Friedburg there is an old castle where the people would make the people coming from the castle where Habbo works pay taxes on salt mined in the Bad Nauheim area. If they didn't pay, they would take their salt. Habbo works in the good castle and I work by the bad castle.

June 27, 1968

It is Thursday evening. Habbo is asleep on the couch, the dogs and the cat are asleep also. Audrey and Jack left on their trip yesterday a.m. Now I get up at 5:45, walk the dogs, fix breakfast and lunch for Habbo, do dishes, etc. and at 9:00 go down to work with Ann Gillis here at the Stars and Stripes Bookstore. I'm not getting paid for this and I can leave anytime, but I like to stay. It will be that much easier when I'm on my own.

The dogs are very old and miss Audrey. Yesterday they lay in front of the door all day waiting for them to come back.

It's amazing to me how fast you get to know people in a place like this. Army people must get very adaptable to old friends leaving and new people coming. Audrey has offered to take us with them on occasional Sunday trips. However, they are going to the Rhine River this Saturday while we are gone.

I've heard from several people that teaching at the schools for dependents would be a discouraging place to start teaching. My job at the book store is very pleasant.

Yesterday afternoon I got myself sort of stranded in Friedburg. I couldn't find anyone at the train station who spoke English, but I've learned to say, "One ticket to_____" in German, so I finally got back after two hours of waiting and a five minute train ride. The trains go very fast here and some stop at every little town. I went to a meeting in Friedburg yesterday, on how to proceed in case the dependents are evacuated. The enemy better be moving slowly if we're to get out before they get here.

This town, Bad Nauheim, is kind of like Aspen—all ready for tourists and so are the prices—but Butzbach is different. Butzbach is full of little shops and narrow streets. There have been people in the area for 6,000 years. However, in about 1100 it was incorporated. The castle where Habbo works was built about

1600. In many places I have seen old ladies with black stockings and old-fashioned clothes. In the country between the towns there are dozens of ladies working in the fields.

I'm glad I'm working. I really felt useless those few days when I didn't know what I'd be doing. They teased me all the time about sleeping so much last week. They said the time difference and the climate change cause that. One day I could hardly stay awake on the bus until we got on the autobahn, and I was almost shaken off the seat. One lane is for trucks and it is very bumpy.

It is true that they drive recklessly over here. On the little streets there may be room for only a car and two baby buggies. All the German babies seem to come out in their buggies every day. G.I.s lose rank, pay, and get in a lot of trouble if they have a car accident.

Monday, July 8, 1968

Habbo and I are at the train station in Giessen and it is 10:00 p.m. We have just returned from visiting his relatives and are waiting for forty-five minutes for a train to Bad Nauheim.

First of all, Habbo's father's father died during the night of July 4-5. His funeral was today. We arrived in Aurich the evening of July 3. We visited with his grandma and aunt, uncle and cousin. His grandma (his mother's mother) looks just like a storybook grandma. She has one cow and one pig. The house and barn are one building.

The morning of July 4, we rode bicycles to see Habbo's grandpa and step-grandmother. They told us he had been asleep since Friday. He was 85. We looked at him as he was sleeping heavily and we stayed for several hours at their house. His two sons by his second wife and also the wife of one of the sons live in the same house.

Friday morning when we got up, Habbo's aunt came over to tell us his step-grandma called and said his grandfather died during the night. The funeral was at 12:30.

They kept his grandfather in the living room in his casket. He was only washed, nothing else. He looked nice. The casket wasn't put in a vault in the ground—just in the dirt. I only met him a few hours before he died but since I was his grandson's wife, they sat me right up front with the closest relatives. I felt kind of out of place, but everyone was real nice and kind of nudged me along.

During the funeral the men and women sit on opposite sides of the church, and I have a hard time of it when I lose my interpreter. There was a large area at the front of the church in front of the pews where the casket was. The family sat on chairs facing the casket—the men on one side and the women on the other. I sat by Habbo's father's only sister and was told to do everything she did since I wouldn't understand what was being said. At one point she got up from her chair, so I did too. She walked toward the casket, so I did too. She had a rose to put on her father's casket, and I realized I should have stayed on my chair. There was nothing to do but follow her back to our chairs. I don't know if anyone knew why I followed her.

It was all nice (if that's a good word to describe such a thing) until we went out to the church cemetery. Then there were about a zillion flies from the decaying flowers, and it started to rain.

Habbo's father received first just a black and white paper announcing the death, which must have been a shock. He won't get any letters until two or three days later, but I guess any way he heard it, it would be a shock.

Afterwards we went back to Habbo's grandma's and that night Habbo's mother's younger sister, her husband, and sixteen-year-old daughter took us up to see the North Sea and we went swimming in a pool by the sea. The water was from the sea but without dead fish. It was dirty and salty and the air was very cold.

The morning we left Bad Nauheim, I discovered my yellow and my white dresses had been stolen off the clothesline. I hope they fit well because they were pretty dresses and I'd hate to see them worn sloppily. Not that I'm bitter or anything. The same morning the cat ate half the cheese and bologna I bought for sandwiches for on the train. Daddy said everything wouldn't always be all rosy.

[Note from 2002: I remember that Uncle Arnulf picked Habbo and me up from the train station in Leer on July 3. He took us to Oma Walle's where she was standing with Tante Netti and Dagmar at the end of the barn in the driveway. They were so nice and friendly. We had tea and strawberry torte right away. This was the first day I met all of them. Habbo had been there in April which was his first time back since his family left Germany in March of 1956.

Gerd Pfeifer, Habbo's cousin on his father's side, took us back to the train station after the funeral on July 8. I met most of the relatives on both sides of the family that very first visit because of the funeral of Habbo's grandfather.

Everyone wore black to the funeral. I had no black clothes so Dagmar's confirmation dress was loaned to me for the funeral. I think a bit of trim had to be taken off of it so it would be appropriate for a funeral. Tante Netti or Dagmar might remember.]

July 11, 1968

I'm waiting for the train because I'm on my way to work. Tuesday night we finally got moved into our apartment. It's nice to have our own place. Yesterday was my first day of working and I like it better than any job I've had because I work by myself yet there are people to talk to. Habbo got moved to a job he likes better, and after August he wouldn't have K.P. However, yesterday he got orders to go to Italy as soon as possible. He wants to leave Monday the 21st. I'll see if they will let me work exactly a month until August 9.

Hopefully that will give Habbo time to find a place for us to live. We will be in the foothills of the Alps and two hours from Innsbruck, Austria and not far from Venice. It's supposed to be the choicest base in Europe and the guys thought Habbo really was lucky, but right now we don't see it that way since things were going so well here. The part we don't like is telling the landlord and my boss. Also, I hope I can find a job down there that's as good as this one, with such good hours.

July 20, 1968

It is Saturday morning, and I'm at work. Habbo will come at 1:00 and we'll take the Rhine trip. Guess what?! Habbo got promoted to E-4 which means $80 more a month. He was very lucky to get it because there were several reasons it would have been logical to not promote him. (Length of time in service, and he's leaving.) It came at a good time since I won't be working for a while when we move. He is supposed to stay in Italy the rest of his time, so we'll have the allotment for me included in his check. After that, you shouldn't have to deal with it.

I have sixteen more days to work here. They have a replacement for me, and last night a couple rented the apartment. So we just won't be missed at all! This is a very nice job, especially for someone who lives close.

July 27, 1968

It is Saturday morning, a beautiful day, and I'm waiting for the train to go to work. If I were an orange thing, I'd come out on a day like this. I'll explain…When we first moved in here and I'd walk through the woods by myself, I would sometimes see these pretty orange seedpods about three inches long. I thought they were kind of pretty and nonchalantly stepped over them. Well, one day when I was walking with Habbo, he asked me if I'd seen them and he touched one with his foot and it started crawling. As seedpods, they were pretty, but as orange crawling things they are as repulsive as snakes to me. He thought I'd be interested because they aren't found in the U.S. They are some kind of snail. So now when I go out, I consider whether many orange things may be lying about in my path. I won't miss them a bit when I leave here tomorrow.

Did I ever mention that Germans almost all seem to have fences, shutters, and locked doors? Here where we live, we have to lock their outside door during the day and they even lock it when they are in the yard. They don't have screens on the windows and there are no storm doors.

I don't think I said much about the Rhine trip. We were very lucky to get to go because there was only one seat left on the bus, and Habbo agreed to sit on a chair in the aisle. We didn't know you had to buy the tickets ahead of time. The boat trip was about three hours. It was gray, cold, and rainy, but we took movies anyway. It has been "unseasonably cold" here all week according to the radio.

[Note from 2002: 1968 was later known as a poor year for German wine because of the cold damp summer.]

July 31, 1968

Boy! I just got two letters from you and two from Habbo.

Audrey and Jack are gone all day and are out for supper, too. I thought I would take advantage of their absence to monopolize the bathroom and while doing that I could put my load of clothes in the washer. Well, I put the clothes and soap in, plugged in this and that, turned knobs, and skipped off to the bathroom to fill the tub for a long, hot bath. I could hear the washer making all its little noises and was satisfied that all was well until I put one foot into the tub. Then I heard the first cycle start to drain, and I realized I hadn't put the hose into the sink! It was just running all over. So I jumped out, ran in the kitchen, but because I was standing in water with the electrical converter I was afraid to touch anything. So I ran and put on my baggy dress and ran across the hall and rang the neighbors' bell (at least I didn't lock myself out). No one answered so I ran back and grabbed the hose and put it in the sink. By then only about a gallon of water was left. I started mopping and the water was heading toward the living room. I didn't stop it from getting to the army's carpet, but I did stop it before it got to Jack and Audrey's own little carpet under the dining room table. Then I proceeded to mop with towels. Ann from upstairs rang the doorbell needing a key to her own apartment because she was locked out. When I showed her what I had done, she just shook her head and left, so I didn't expect any help. I went on mopping, and wringing, and thinking I should have stayed home. Then the doorbell rang again and there stood Ann with her mop! We mopped, vacuumed, and waxed and cleaned up the stuff we used to clean up. She said the place looked 49% better than before the flood.

A little while ago Audrey came home for a minute to walk the dogs. I told her about the water and she just said, "Did you mop it up?" I said I had and she said, "Good."

Did I tell you about when I stayed here before and one of their dogs kept me in the bathroom for more than an hour just by growling outside the door? I have an awful time with her. That's why I don't walk them. I've tried. I waited in the bathroom as all the different kinds of accents went up and down the stairs. Well, I could finally hear Ann (from Mississippi) and Gil (from Boston), so I yelled at them to come in and get Tessie away so I could come out. They sent their four-year-old son in first and thought it was real funny. Now they can tell about the flood, too.

The "nice dog" is lying right here beside my bed. I like her. Then there's also the cat. When I had their living room carpet turned back to dry, he clawed chunks of the spongy stuff off the back so I put him in the room I stay in and shut the door. He took a nap on my light blue dress and left his hair.

Habbo's letters said the scenery in Switzerland was beautiful, the housing situation is better than here, his job fine, weather like Iowa but more rain, and swimming close by.

I'm glad, of course, to hear Lucy is well and you had a good trip. Write more about it now that you are back. I'm happy that you saw Habbo's parents and they you.

Habbo's relatives and everyone else thinks Mama looks very young and pretty. Dagmar, Habbo's sixteen-year-old cousin, thought Daddy looked very "American." I, being one, don't recognize the quality or qualities which make one look "very American."

August 9, 1968

I'm in Vicenza at the railway station waiting for Habbo. When I first arrived, after I realized he wasn't here, I was really discouraged because I don't have a little Italian book, and I don't even know how to say, "Thank you." I told the information lady I would be here if Habbo arrives. I bought a coke and I'm sipping very slowly so I can stay here.

I told Habbo I was sure I would be arriving Saturday, August 10 at 10:00 a.m. Maybe he took me at my word, although he had told me to try to leave last night because the trains would be much less crowded. It's good that I did because they were crowded anyway.

The trip was about sixteen hours and the two people in my compartment were Italian. We all spoke a bit of German so that's how we communicated. I changed trains in Milan and the train from there to here was packed shoulder to shoulder. At every stop, I asked "Vicenza" in a questioning voice. The people in my compartment all shook their heads at the same time. When we finally arrived in Vicenza, they all made it clear that it was my destination!

The temperament of the people is different than in Germany. They were much more reserved. The people here are much more open and shout at each other from the train. That was rare where we were in Germany.

Mr. Schalk, where I stayed in Friedberg, gave me a yellow, a red, and a pink rose to give to Habbo from them. They were very nice people and want us to write. It has to be in German. Those people and many people in Germany don't mind asking how much anything costs. Mrs. Schalk wanted to know how much my ticket was, and I was really doing the best I could to tell her, but she couldn't understand. Finally, she pointed to my purse and wanted to know if it wasn't in there. When I got the ticket out, she saw that it was from Bad Nauheim instead of Friedberg, and she didn't think they would let me on the train with it. Habbo said as long as you got on someplace closer to your destination, it was perfectly okay. I was only losing about fifteen cents.

I couldn't get Mrs. Schalk to understand that it didn't matter, so she insisted on going with me in the rain in the dark to make sure they let me on the train. She seemed happy to do it, and she carried my little bag of fruit and the three roses.

From what I can see this looks like a clean, pretty town. It reminds me of Washington state because I could see water and low mountains. Going through Switzerland was pretty.

Later

It has been about six hours since I started waiting for Habbo. The army people told me he moved out of the barracks yesterday, and they gave me his address. I took a taxi there and am waiting on the steps. However, the girl downstairs says the apartment is empty and I don't know if that's true or if she just hasn't seen Habbo yet. I think I'll wait until after dark, and if he doesn't come, I'll take a taxi back to the train station and wait there all night. I hate to think of that. I don't know whether to be mad at myself for telling him I didn't think I could be here yet, be mad at him for encouraging me to come and then being so hard to find, or to sit and worry about him. So I do all three and feel sorry for myself. Perhaps he changed his mind about this apartment and is busy finding another one or maybe he got an opportunity to go someplace and didn't think I would be here already.

August 10, 1968
4:00 p.m.

Last night I went back to the train station at 8:00. Train stations are easy to find once you find the tracks! I called the post again and this time Habbo came. It's a long story about why they didn't find him. For one thing, I neglected to say I was his wife when I called the first time, and I guess that was an important bit of information. It was an Italian holiday and Habbo was playing tennis because he gets off work for American and Italian holidays.

I was at the right apartment. It is really nice. There are three rooms in a row with the bedroom being closest to the street. There is a long hall and a bathroom and a separate toilet.

We have hot water in the bathroom! I don't think we'll use the sitting room much except for storing things. The apartment is downtown, upstairs on the third floor. It is clean, and so is the street even though the buildings are old. It is a busy place, but I feel like we have more privacy. It certainly is a different atmosphere (outside) than where we were in Germany.

The gas won't be hooked up until Monday morning, so we can't cook or use the water heater. The army refrigerator will be moved in then, too.

There is a wardrobe in the bedroom and sitting room and a hutch in the kitchen. I don't see what more we could ask for. It's really nice and everything is so convenient! Habbo says the job situation looks pretty good for me, too. Either teaching or, if not, the man who runs the commissary said there might be an opening there. I would like some kind of teaching job so I can start doing something about my fear of it.

I wish you could see how it is here. If Willie comes next summer, he could sleep in the sitting room. We do plan ahead!

The weather is perfect. I saw where Habbo works and it is very nice too. Tonight we're going to walk around and look at Vicenza. There are several old famous buildings here. I wish I had those two sleeveless dresses. They were cooler than the ones I have left, but I'll survive. I like the smell of warm air. Remind me never to complain about heat again.

August 12, 1968

Habbo just left to pick up the last of our things at the train station. He'll also bring home groceries we bought today. A friend is helping him with an army jeep. Then it looks like we are pretty well set as soon as I find out what to do with the garbage. The army brought our refrigerator this morning. It's a brand new big one. It's beautiful. Habbo had to hook it up, though, and that was a four hour project. The wiring is different than in Germany and we brought two German transformers with us and the refrigerator is American. Somehow he got it going, but next time I think I'll take a long walk when he gets involved in a do-it-himself project.

I bought some canisters, a mop, a dust mop, and clothespins this morning. That was fun! There are four little clotheslines out the kitchen window. They run along the building to the sitting room window, and I can pull the clotheslines back and forth on a pulley.

August, 14, 1968

I think it will be nice to be in the same place for a while and be able to plan ahead and have a hazy idea about what is happening next. I talked to the principal at the elementary school on the post and he sounded very encouraging. I have to fill out a lot of papers and go back at 10:00 tomorrow morning and he will interview me. He asked what I would think of being an assistant to the special education teacher. I think I would like that. Anyway, he sounded as though they would have something because they have a shortage of teachers here. It's unbelievable how well things are going.

I used Easy Off to clean the oven. It still doesn't work, but it looks nice. The stove has four burners. The one in Germany had two. Four burners will be nice because we have to heat dishwater. We unplug the hot water heater except at bath time because electricity, water, and gas are very expensive here.

We have our first mosquito bites. There aren't any screens here, just as in Germany. I have to open the windows sometimes. All the windows have shutters which everyone uses because there are no blinds, shades, or storm windows.

Habbo discovered this morning that we have new neighbors or old ones returned from vacation. The man is also a German citizen in the American army. He lives with his Italian girlfriend. He gave Habbo a ride to work this morning, so Habbo was able to use his German again.

August 15, 1968

I just returned from my interview. He said they will definitely use me as a substitute and we should get a phone. The pay is $22.50 per day, and you get paid every two weeks. They call about 7:45 in the morning and school starts at 8:30 and lasts until 2:30. Teachers are free to leave at 3:00.

The principal said teachers pick the kids up out on the playground and take them to the classrooms in the morning. I'll be sworn in in the morning. I'm going to go back to the post and eat lunch with Habbo. Going back and forth is so easy here. I went there just to buy aluminum foil Tuesday. The bus just goes around and around every few minutes.

August 19, 1968

Yesterday we went to Lake Garda. It's very big, and it is about as far west from here as Venice is east. Everything but the food is free. The Service Club has made a very nice place there. They have boat rides and water skiing. We took a boat ride, but the lake was too choppy for skiing yesterday.

When I arrived here last weekend, Habbo was telling me the merits of buying a Fiat and selling the Chevy. Two days later we received a letter from Pat offering to buy it if we wanted to sell it. Could you tell us how much '62 Chevys are worth?

Today at 1:00 I have my physical for school and I'll be all done getting qualified to teach. It is a civil service job and the FBI checks up on me yet.

[Note from 2002: My mother told me her store manager for whom I had also worked received a call or visit from the FBI about me.]

We still have to get a phone, which will take a while because we have to talk to the landlady who is away on vacation and also there is a waiting list for having phones installed. Our water has been shut off for three days because it leaks downstairs. It is supposed to be fixed today.

Next week—Monday through Friday—Habbo will be out in the field. Just about everyone on the post goes. Five days won't be very long. I'm glad it doesn't include any Sundays.

I realize I am very fortunate to be here, and everything is just fine. I want to take full advantage of our opportunities to see other places. I'll have to look forward to sending and receiving pictures until I can see you for real.

August 21, 1968

Monday night the couple next door came over to visit. They told us that Romeo and Juliet's castle is near here even though Shakespeare wrote the play to take place in Verona, which isn't far from here either. The real Romeo and Juliet lived long before Shakespeare wrote the play, but what happened to them in the play was a real incident near here.

There is a chess game played near Romeo's castle. It's a big chess game in the town square, which they play every two years. Real people are the chess "pieces." The first time it was played so all the people could watch as two men played against each other and the one who won could marry the princess.

It makes us happy to get letters from home. I'm glad some of my relatives were born in Frankfurt because we plan to go through there at Christmas. I didn't see much of it while we were in Germany. I hope we can stop by a couple of Catholic churches and see if they let just anyone look through their records of births.

August 26, 1968

Habbo left for the field this morning and will be back Friday night. I just talked to the girl downstairs (with the help of our neighbors) and it's okay for the school to call there if I'm needed to substitute. A phone would be very expensive and would take months of waiting, so we aren't getting one.

Yesterday we took the train to Venice. A railroad and highway are built side by side on a strip of land through the water to Venice. Everyone walks or goes by boat from there. We went by boat down the Grand Canal to St. Mark's Square. We window shopped, ate, and watched the people.

August 27, 1968

I like to look out the window that faces the street. It has just turned dark and it is very warm and humid. There is a sidewalk next door. There are people walking by. A lady across the street was standing out on her balcony. Trucks and other noisy vehicles go by until about 11:00 p.m. and our windows rattle.

When you look out that window to the left, the river is a block away. Six busy streets come together there, and the streets are narrow here in the central old part of town.

Today I bought a cake pan because Habbo figured out how to light the oven. There is a fruit store near us and Habbo brings some home almost every night.

I'm glad you had fun on your vacation. How is Ann's turtle? Does she still poke his appendages back in? It's fun to watch the little kids in the square here feed and chase the pigeons. I saw a little girl go by on the front of her mother's bicycle the other day, and she had on a straw hat and sunglasses. It seemed like she should know me, but she looked very serious and went on by.

It seems as though even more people ride bicycles here than in Germany. Perhaps the weather is more suited to it year-round. I guess we will soon find out. It doesn't seem like summer should be almost over.

Letters From America

By Lisa Fokkena

April 4, 2002

Dear Laura, Erika, Lisa, and Laurel,

Aahhh!!!

I broke down in Julesburg, Colorado!!!!

Help!! Well, okay, there's nothing you can do to help, but, ahhhh!!

It's a tiny little town where they're all unfriendly if you haven't lived here for the last twenty years and tried to "fit in." (You see, if you don't try to "fit in" they don't like you anyway, even if you are a local.)

I was in a big rush to make Abbie's birthday party tonight, and "chill with the homies" but there's no way now. Erg! Thank goodness for the joint I didn't throw out in a fit of paranoia. Almost did.

Now I'm stuck here, and eventually the guy might get around to attempting to fix the damn belt, or whatever it is. I should have told him "MY FRIEND IS IN LABOR, I'VE GOT TO HURRY!!" But who knows if that would have helped.

The lady behind the desk was even bitchy when I inquired as to how long it might take. I had to say (upbeat, happy tone) "oh, that's fine, everything's positive and happy" for her to lose her bitchy thing. She began with giving me an estimate, at which point I said, "Oh, no, I don't care about that, I want to know how long it will take." That statement in itself is going to cost me $100 more than it would have been. Because that's how the system works.

Remember in Olympia, when I went to suavely open my car hood, to prove that I know something about cars, and couldn't get it? And, yup, that one cost me another twenty bucks. Turns out (I think) they didn't even fix the belt that time. Sheesh.

And if it is my timing belt, I've heard you can make those work temporarily with nylons. Wish I knew a little more about cars and wore pantyhose.

Oh! Also, in this pleasant little town, I was walking down to the main street to find food and the library, when I almost stepped on a dead bird on the sidewalk. Rock! And then on the way back to the car place, I almost stepped on a damn MOUSE dead in a parking lot. Elch. I'm taking a different route on the way back. See what else I can find.

Also, I haven't mentioned to the place, that, uh, I don't have any money. I've got forty bucks in the debit system, which I am planning to use all at once quick to fill up on gas and whatnot on the way home. It seems that the computers don't process all that quickly in time to catch me, and decline the action. And I have fourteen dollars cash in my pocket. I'm leaving the bill part for the end, and hopefully someone will help me out somehow over the phone.

Good grief.

I hope I'm taking care of all the breakdown karma for the year for all of us in this one event.

Good luck, happier driving than I've had today, love from the Colorado/ Nebraska border.

5 May, 2002. 10:41 am.

Okay, where to start??

I left off in Charleston. Retrospectively, I was the "hillbilly" in West Virginia. I don't know where it got its bad rap. Probably from tourists like myself. Everyone was really nice. And other than their slightly funny way of talking—which was overshadowed by the "folks" in Kantuckiii—they were perfectly normal and refined. Maybe I missed something.

Example of me being a hick:

I stopped at a roadside market to buy something, and mainly to talk to "them there folks" (which was my preconceived impression, therefore not really an impression, etc., etc.) in hopes of getting a better feel for the West Virginian mentality.

Well, I bought my grapes. Seedless. That was my self-created ordeal. "Are you SURE there aren't any seeds in there?"

So, no seeds, and dammit, only one pound, which was $1.50.

It came to $1.59 but hey, nine cents, that's okay.

After he weighed it out, and gave me my change, I asked if I could buy one strawberry—they were huge, red, and really juicy-looking—so he handed me one, and I asked "how much more is that?" beyond the 1.59 right?

He replied, "You can just have it," sort of condescending, but with more pity for my lack of class or something. Who knows.

So, I get in my car, and take a bite of the strawberry.

God! It was good.

As I was driving away, I pointed to the strawberry, smiled real big, and gave him a thumbs up.

And I'm not the hick?

Yes, yes, that was me.

From there the border to Kentucky was near.

I get to Kentucky, I'm tired and grumpy, agonizing over recent boy issues. I find a campground, and after checking the hot water temperature, and whether or not it really is hot, I go with it. Ten dollars. Me, my tent, and one night. No firewood, thanks.

All's well until the next morning, while naked in the shower, partway through the conditioning, I realize that HOLY FUCK! there's a frog watching me. Not even watching me from the floor, across the room, but right there next to me, crotch level on the wall. Hanging there by its grotesque little suction-cup hands. The spiderman of frogdom.

I survived by pretending that my child was with me and I had to prove that it didn't bother me, so I wouldn't pass along any unnecessary phobias to my off-spring—i.e. Laura with the worm in the garden. Hold it, pretend you like it, so Rakaya knows that it's okay to befriend worms, and won't spend the rest of her life freaking out if she sees one.

The day progressed. La di da. Kentucky.

I got on the turnpike, crossing my fingers that it wouldn't be as expensive as New York's, or as frequent as Chicago's. When I finally did approach a booth, about twenty miles into it (good distance) the woman waved me on…what's this? I was handing her the fifty cents (good price) but she said the guy ahead of me had paid for me. "Something about you look like a million bucks"??!!!?? (Don't forget to imagine her accent.)

What??

Cool!

But, what??

"Whatever" and "rock on" were the emotions I went with.

Then as the second booth came, I wondered if he would do it again, that would save me a total of a much needed dollar, and *bygolly* he did!

But at this point, I, like, owe him a buck, so therefore owe him something, maybe not a blowjob yet, but a stroke of the ego definitely.

I solved it all with style and grace by passing him, letting him follow for a while, and then taking an obvious gas station exit. At which point I flail my arm out the window in thanks, and he honks his semi horn, and all ends quite well and happy.

Onto? Great Conversationalists in Kentucky.

I swear I overheard:

A woman in reference to her son: "Yup, that's he. He's all growed up!"

Man bumping into me in store (imagine the chuckling of one of those looney toon cartoons): "Well, I almost rund you over!"

Every time someone would talk to me I would run back to the car giggling hysterically. I could never be in a bad mood in Kentucky. Or have a serious conversation, either.

Sunday night I gave up on the expensive campground I had found fifty miles east of Nashville and went the cheaper, more educational route of "Fuck it! I'm going to town!"

And I did.

I met a lovely woman, first time meeting a woman in a bar, and spent the evening talking to a her, rather than a him. That was brilliant, and she gave me all sorts of useful information about random relevant issues to my life. Womyn's Festival in Michigan, female artists, and whatnots all around. I'm excited, and my interest is growing in areas that had been growing dim as of late. (Stupid boy problems.)

I leave Nashville, and find a campground with the help of a woman who, outright, struck up a conversation mid-pee at a truck stop. Who would have ever thunk? She directed me to a couple of sites, but then I was forced to hear the whole "I can't believe you're alone!" followed by "How old are you?" and then the "Do your parents know what you're doing?"

I escaped mostly unscathed, and found the site.

I slept.

Woke up dreaming of a tornado hitting Clarksville. (Not the one in Tennessee, the one in Iowa, ha! When am I ever going to be able to conversationally make that distinction again?)

Woke up, took a shower, everything was fine until I was brushing my teeth. The water smelled funny. I even smelled the water. (Ewww, you think?) Then as I'm on my third-to-last spit, something, I still don't know what kind that was, crawled right on up out of the drain. It looked like a roach, but it was more neon blue, and twice the size of a healthy New Yorker. I grabbed my shit and ran.

That brings you up to date, save the frisbee golf sort of way I found this computer. I stopped five times to ask directions, and I am not exaggerating, I don't know how I'm going to find the highway again. Good Christ, I kept getting closer, and closer, but never quite there. I'm in Athens, Alabama. God bless 'em.

6 May, 2002. 10:39 am.

Ahaaaaa.

Left off in somewhere in northern Alabama. Sweet home…no, wait, no way. I did at one point sit on the porch of a gas station, though. That seemed so appropriate! I was drinking apple juice though, rather than tea. Same color.

Not much new has happened. I drove, drove, drove yesterday, 500+ miles. Too paranoid to smoke, so no new profound thoughts. Other than the ongoing debate within my mind about whether or not the word "noun" could be an adjective.

When I got to the exit where I had planned to camp there were no signs anywhere beside the road advertising campgrounds. On the map it said there were five. I drove down the road towards where they should have been, until I freaked out whilst driving over a bridge that I was convinced would falter while I was on it (my recurring nightmare as a child) so I ditched the camping for a night, and got a hotel. They should really give discounts to broke traveling people such as myself. Especially for low quality hotels as the one I ended up in. But I survived it. And hey! It had air conditioning, too!

It's so humid that get this, my hair is actually *curling*. That has never, ever happened before. It seems to be slinking up around the edges. It's too bizarre. For my head, anyway.

I'm on to New Orleans! Anne Rice, Trent Reznor, and all things vampire! Claudia, Louis, and Lestat, here I come! Tombs above ground (actually, aren't all tombs above ground? or at least accessible without digging through dirt?), rats the size of dogs, and scary people down winding alleys!

I even practiced flashing myself in the mirror, and hey! Not that bad! I have always been so un-confident about that sort of thing. I just happen to have the right jeans and tank top on. I think I can pull this off once I have a belt on. Then the love handles should be tucked, and no bra makes an easier flash. I've never flashed anyone before. Might take me a coupla beers.

I have my cape along, too! But that just doesn't go with the outfit. I think that's an unwritten law. "Don't wear your cape with denim." Unless it's a denim cape. Would that ever catch on? I hope not.

Almost out of Mississippi, one hour 'til the city. My offer to accept a hotel room overlooking Bourbon Street still stands.

Prost!

7th May, 2002. 10:37 am.

Where is a sugar daddy when I need one? People buy you beers, but no one ever buys your time at the internet cafe.

I'm in "Nawlins"! At an internet cafe, six bucks for half an hour, fuck! There goes the enjoyment of saving a buck from the tolls.

I read my map all the way into town, trying to figure out where the French Quarter was, and, lo and behold, there are actual signs from the interstate directing a tourist towards it. I ended up parking on Toulouse and Bourbon, which I hear, from the first person I talked to anyway, is a pretty good place to be.

So I park, and I'm gesturing to a guy sipping on his Tall Boy on the step. "Is this okay to park here?" He was very cool, and even tried to avert the meter reading lady as she gave me a ticket while I was calling the friend—supposed to meet me, where is she?—and peeing. Too late. I now owe Louisiana $20 for ill-parking in their city.

But that can be paid later, right?

Post-ticket, I sat on the stoop for awhile with Tyrell, I think his name was, very cool, nice guy.

I stumbled down Bourbon Street after this, and found a place called the Blues Bar on Bourbon. I probably got that wrong, but I've had a few. Turned out to be a club where they encourage the women to get up and "shake their rumps" on the stage. Not my gig.

I found a nice live jazzy band after that and shot the shit with the piano player and a guy from Mississippi. And now I found a great bagel (they had sprouts!) and an internet cafe. But this costs money, so gotta go!

8th May, 2002. 8:02 pm.

Whew. *wipes brow* I escaped.

Slightly scathed this time, but I've decided to leave the true gore of my night in New Orleans out. No details for nobody. I'll just tuck that one in my pocket and continue on.

I did, though, get the coolest fucking hotel room ever. $68.43. The guy went as low as $60, but I guess there was tax-n-stuff. I could have thrown a rock from the entrance and hit Bourbon Street. It was the grooviest hotel room I've had. So Roman. It had a balcony that overlooked the courtyard (and pool) and beyond the skyline of the French Quarter buildings there was the skyscraper skyline. Very very very cool! And it was a four poster bed with the connecting beams. Just incredible! It created a slight dilemma though. Since I had such a great room I just wanted to hang out there, but the point of me having it was so I would have a safe place to go back to post-drinking. Finally I dragged myself out of it and I took on the town with gusto.

I sat for about five beers at one bar watching a blues-y cover band. Quite nice. A drunken Irish man hit on me, and I hit on the saxophone player.

I ended up hanging out with a guy named Attila. We went to a beer garden and I had a hurricane. Eventually he went home, and I hung out with a man I met in the downtown area (where I *did* flash my tits! *high fives self*) and I threw in the towel about three a.m.

Now I'm hung over and avoiding the self-loathing that comes after a night of heavy drinking. It's muggy out.

I'm going to camp in Pensacola. Because I'm a dork, and that's where Jodie Foster's character ended up in outer space (Contact) and Joan Osborne sings about it and a trailer in the sand. "Well, I found him, in Pensacola, in a trailer in the sand…have you come to take the car away, I don't have it anymore…….'"

10th May, 2002. 8:04 pm.

Seen on tip jars in New Orleans:

New Orleans—
party,
vomit,
go home.

And:

Tip your bartenders,
we know voodoo.

11th May, 2002. 8:04 pm.

Now I am a bit more than one hour from Orlando! Which is going to become the cumulative end of my journey forward. I'm on my last fifty dollars, and am going to have to start Sissy Hankshaw-ing it, rather than Bill Bryson-ing it. This leaves me without Delaware. Forever more (until I make a special trip to Dover, but who vacations there?) I will have to say, "I've been to forty-eight states." Then, of course, people will assume "Oh? Everywhere but Alaska and Hawaii?" Then I'll be forced to explain, "No, you see…" and that will just annoy me.

Unless of course someone wants to buy a Volkswagen Jetta. It's red. And a diesel. But I want it back when it dies to make a flower pot.

Wish me resourceful luck!

13th May, 2002. 8:06 pm.

Ahhhhhh….. *big sigh*

I have reclaimed my happy wonderful perspective on life that, I think, just maybe, might be attached to sunny warmer climates.

But, more so, I think that it has to do with the attitudes of the people I am surrounded by. I am so affected by who is around me.

My weekend in Orlando rawked!

Sharon and Paco were splendid to hang out with, talk to, and they were great guides. Well, Sharon was. Paco left for Puerto Rico Saturday morning, and hosted the gaming tables Friday night, so most of the time was spent hanging with her. Marvelous, marvelous woman!

Saturday we went to the Kennedy Space Center. And! The visitor center was open! We got to go in and check things out, which makes life come full circle, because we met at the Star Trek bar in Las Vegas. They need to have a Star Trek experience outside of the entrance, somewhere near Space Camp (I got to see the Space Camp building) because, hey, you don't like one without the other! Same with every other nerdy science place in the world; they need Trekkie bars near them. Like a Hooters near a porn shop or something, but I think that might be a bad analogy.

We went to a tiki bar near Cocoa Beach.

Fact: a tiki bar is an open bar with a thatched sort of roof. That's what makes it tiki. Or, at least, this is my understanding.

It was totally groovy, and just what I thought Florida should be. It was packed with people drinking pink slushy drinks. There was a band playing popular covers, people dancing, and a woman with a veil. How very Caribbean.

Sunday was Mother's Day and her (amazing, charismatic, very cool) daughter made us pancakes and took us to a movie. That was great, but I wondered the whole time if I was intruding on their time together. I think it was okay, though. They're both so nice. Later in the evening we went out for a piña coloda, and that made my Florida experience complete.

Right now I am in St. Augustine, the oldest town in the U.S. or North America or something. (Didn't make it to the museum with the facts. I should get a brochure so I sound educated.) Heading for a camping site somewhere in South Carolina, and tomorrow I'll go see the woman I met in Nashville. Life is so fun!

But I'm straggling a bit to get back up on the wagon after the wine last night, so the clever wittiness shall come later.

While I'm in Florida still: "Later, gator!"

How's that for sharp wit?

15th May, 2002. 8:06 pm.

I'm back in good ol' West Virgin-eeya, being the hick that I am in this state.

I'm in Princeton at the library. There is the cutest boy working the desk. So helpful and nice! And awful-gosh-cute!

Where was I last?

St. Augustine…

Since then I drove to Raleigh. Which was pretty uneventful until I talked to Mom and realized that she forgot about putting the other half of the $ in the account (I received my birthday cash early this year) which left me with twenty bucks in South Carolina. Not to mention a faulty gas gauge. It chronically stated <—of E.

I had to figure out a way to sleep in my tent, and eat Tuesday while on the road to Raleigh, and I might possibly need gas, but I really couldn't tell, because the—

Fuck!

The cute guy just commented to some old guy, "I used to travel; I've been to every state except Alaska and Hawaii. And I'm only twenty."

Swear-to-god I just heard that.

A year ago today I left for Alaska. And as of yesterday, I've been to forty-eight states too. Does that make him or me cooler? I should ask him out for coffee or a bagel. Maybe this is Lisa's soul mate, right here in southern West Virginia. We could just buy a house and have nine kids right now. No travel necessary, it's already been done.

Humph.

Back to no money in North Carolina.

I survived by the skin of a penny. Or something to that effect.

I got away at the campground with only paying ten dollars of the eighteen I owed. I offered to hang out all day until the cash processed. After I bought a Mt. Dew and a (over-fucking-priced) subway deli style cheese sandwich I had one dollar bill, and change. I finally had to break down and buy gas (break down of my resolve, not the car) and with my change I had $2.03 counting every penny.

At which point I began the infamous "car scrounge."

And woo boy! That shit works!

I had thought it wouldn't produce much since I'd scoured and vacuumed prior to packing up the car, but I even found *quarters!* I did the floor first, and found about eighty cents, whooping every time I found a quarter. Then I proceeded to the luggage where I knew I might have tossed loose change while emptying my pockets at various points. And then on to the only place left I could think of, which was the glove box, and! There were four quarters in there!

All in all, added up, I had found $2.66! Which gave me $4.69 in gas—3.5 some gallons, which is 100+ miles in my car.

I hung out at the library for two hours waiting for the friend to get done working. After about an hour of being online and reading a book in the back, I noticed a sign on the wall: "Volunteers needed." So, what the hell? I went up to the desk, explained that I was just passing through, chilling there until my friend got off work, and would they like me to shelve some books in the meantime? I'm, like, able, you know? I did that for a week in Steamboat Springs. I know how the Dewey Decimal System works.

But no, she declined my offer.

"There's a lot of paperwork to go through; it wouldn't be worth it."

Hrmph for the second time.

I met the friend and her girlfriend; they were totally cool, gracious, and kind. She took me out to eat (mmm! awesome soup!) and we went for a coupla beers. It was great conversation and perspective. Raleigh seems like a groovy town if you're into the white collar business thing. Or a student. I guess it is the capital, and smaller capital/college towns are like that (i.e. Olympia, Santa Fe, and Columbus too, maybe; I'll find out more tonight).

I took off driving into the night then. (I did only have 2.5 beers. It's legal.) I crashed in my car (fell asleep, didn't wreck anything) around four a.m. (Eastern). Now I'm in a town in West Virginia, heading to Columbus to Ken's.

24th July, 2002. 9:54 pm.

"They have feelings, too, even though they're guys."

—Mom

I wonder if anywhere there is a speed limit that is not a multiple of five?

26th July, 2002. 8:07 pm.

I've got a pot to piss in!

I actually peed in a coffee canister last night! Haha! There's too much light to go outside my tent and pee in the grass (neighbors) and it's a long walk to the bathroom (I'm already half asleep, and I gotta pee!). Aren't I resourceful?!

29th July, 2002. 8:01 pm.

On another note, do you know how much crap I get when I respond "no" to *"Ya gotta man?"* And then they think that I must be "looking" and wonder if they can be "it" for me. The only other single woman I know in the area is not really in the area, she's in Flint, and that's a ways off. She finally achieved a divorce. She initially got married because the guy proposed and then held a gun to his head until she said yes. I don't like the word "weird," but some of the male people here are weird.

16th July, 2002. 8:11 pm.

I bought a hammer today! I think I crossed the boundary into grown-up-hood.

I've already used it three times, once to pry up the tent stakes, once to hammer in the tent stakes (so technically that's eight times, there being four stakes holding my tent to the earth), and the third (or ninth, depending on how one looks at it) to knock on wood when I needed to knock.

It cost $6.29 but came to $6.65, so there must be a thirty-six cent tax on a hammer. Which I think is stupid. The entire thing should have been free. Everyone should get one free hammer in life.

This is the most liberating feeling I've had since February when I pushed my first shopping cart around the supermarket. Prior I'd always gone the basket route, because I just didn't merit all the space of a cart, but this one day I started dropping shit, and there was an abandoned cart, so I took it and I was practically kicking up my heels as I pushed it around the store. What an amazing feeling!

2nd August, 2002. 9:56 pm.

Michigan is the only state where I've noticed billboards for funeral homes and cremation services.

29th August, 2002. 9:55 pm.

Did I just get free gynecology because I knew someone?

12th September, 2002. 9:37 pm.

I always reaffirm to myself (while out of Iowa) that my lifestyle right now couldn't support a child—living in a tent, working sixty-five hours a week, living where I don't know anyone, living in a girl's dorm, working at a seasonal resort living in a cabin, sleeping in my car, etc., etc., but here in Iowa, well, right now there is no reason not to. I've even thought this through. I have my family for when I want to go out, or need a sitter for whatever reason, and even two sets of relatives right here in Cedar Falls for going to class. Not that I want infants this instant, I'm not even done roaming the earth yet, but at the moment, I feel so damn settled, like I should or something.

Creepy thoughts.

2nd October, 2002. 9:56 pm.

I don't think love should be a calculated thing. Preferably it would be a free-flowing emotion that doesn't necessarily make sense, but yet you know it's there and adhere to the call of it.

~Lisa

Left: Onno Fecht and Laura Fokkena at the Kukelorum in Rahe. Before telephones, the Kukelorum—which means "watch and listen"—was a station next to a canal. Those who worked there spent their days watching for ships, and had the job of lugging open the drawbridge whenever they passed. Today the Kukelorum is a small pub with live music every Wednesday night. Summer, 2003.

Below: Gerrit Fecht and Lisa Fokkena at a "Stadtfest" (city-wide party) in Aurich. Summer, 2003.

Poetry Is Yummy, Or The Parable Of The Boy Who Was Made To Drink Beer

By Ray Brost

Medford, Wisconsin, about 1942

A certain man had a young son. Upon this son fell the task of keeping clean his father's repair shop. And in this shop there laboured beside the father two hired servants. One was Buby Krause, and the other of the two was Kris Krueger, the seed of Christopher Krueger. Buby Krause was jolly, and his belly was full and round. Kris Krueger was skinny, and his jowl was full and round with tobacco. Upon this tobacco he did waste his spital. And the son was angry with this servant, for he did spit his cud upon the floor; therefore swept the son together much spital and many cuds. And when it was summer, and the father and his servants had laboured long and well, and the day was declining, the son was called, and the father said unto him, *Son, take this vessel and bring hither from yon Medford Brewery, a measure of beer for two-bits, for we have laboured long and well, and are thirsty and fain to drink.* And when the son was come, the father called together his servants that they might make merry. And he divided unto them the beer, and he spake and said, *We have beer enough and to spare; Son, drink also of this beer, for thou hast swept long and well, and kept clean my repair shop.* The son was exalted, for although he was but a mere youth, he was hence like a man. And he did drink of the beer, yea, and it tasted sour and strange and strong, and he was wont not to swallow it. But he feared to be abased, and so he did persevere.

And thereafter were manifold the times that he did imbibe. The son kept the bidding of his father, from his youth up, and he grew to like beer, and then he grew to love it. And it came to pass that he became a most just and knowing judge of beer. Throughout the kingdom, men entreated him and said: *Meister, we know thou sayeth and teacheth rightly, taste thou of this beer, and prithee tell us, Is it Pilsner, or Export, or Budweiser, or Muenchner Hell?* So he did taste of the beer, and then he beheld them, saying unto them, *Ye know me, and ye know whence I am. Lo, this beer is not from Mexico, nor cometh it from Bavaria or Minnesota. It is Bremer Export, and will set you back three-and-twenty bucks a case!* The people marvelled at his answer and held their peace.

Now, students, it is written that poetry is a nurturing libation that ye should pleasurably ingest. Liken ye it not unto tobacco, which is such that ye spit it out again. Verily, verily I say unto you, if at first, poetry doth not lie well upon your tongues, sip it and quaff it and tipple it in spite of yourselves; persist and endure and be single of purpose; and with the passage of time, ye shall be knowing, and be imbued of its qualities, and ye shall love it, as ye love your CDs and your DVDs, which do fill your abodes.

Church

By Habbo Fokkena

Going to church must be an American invention. In Germany we did not go to church. Like most Germans, we were automatically enrolled at baptism, were confirmed as part of the regular school day, and were thereafter considered good members of the faith. Germans even have money withheld automatically from their paychecks to support their church. No one thinks about it. There are two Christian churches, the *Evangelische Kirche* and the *Katholische Kirche*. Nothing else concerning religion is prominent in daily life.

But Amerika is a hotbed of churches. Every possible denomination or variety is present. And they are present in every small town. When we arrived in Shell Rock in 1956, my parents were absolutely amazed to find a town of 1,300 had seven churches. Seven! And they all seemed to foster regular attendance. If they got too big, or someone got mad at the minister, or took issue with a matter of faith, they split up.

We were immediately adopted by such a splinter group. How this happened, I have no idea. I suspect one our neighbors got us involved. Or—more likely—it was due to the fact that my father got his first job building a church, while we were waiting to move to the farm. Always a pragmatist (a trait my children have not inherited), he probably figured it made sense to go to the church that fed you.

So we started going to church. We first met in a funeral parlor, since our group had splintered from another Lutheran denomination and had no building of its own. We sat on folded chairs, listened to words we did not understand, and tried to sing songs that were equally cryptic. But we went. Unlike in Germany, attendance was expected.

This was new to us, although pastors in Ostfriesland, and in fact all over Germany, were highly respected. When they came to visit a home—which was seldom—they didn't sit in the kitchen, where any other visitor would be expected to sit, but in a special room that is never used except when the pastor comes to call. I can still remember Oma Walle's special room in her farmhouse, with new furniture, white curtains: totally unused. I suspect it was opened when Opa died, since a minister would have been present. Or, it would be used if someone married. But never for anything else.

In fact, I seem to remember staying in her house when I returned to Germany as an adult and thinking it strange to have a room one entered through her bedroom, with brand new furniture and no signs of usage. But, to be an upstanding middle class citizen in Germany, there was always this "gute Stube."

American farmhouses generally did not have such rooms, or I do not recall them. Perhaps the richer farmers adopted the custom and had such rooms hidden in their houses. But I never saw one, probably because I did not become a minister.

But pastors held a powerful sway over their congregation. In Iowa the old ones could speak fluent German; they would visit once a year and were treated like royalty. They had little money, since the Germans never paid their ministers much, but they had influence.

I recall Pastor Matthias, now in his 90s, telling me of the time he and the synod president visited my great-grandfather, Wilhelm. This must have been in the 1940s or early 1950s. Pastor Matthias said that the kitchen had a wood-burning stove and no wallpaper, and he was amazed to hear his boss tell my great-grandfather that this kitchen wasn't good enough for my great-grandmother. *"Wilhelm, you must buy her some wallpaper, and better furniture."* And, lo and behold, at their next visit, the house sported new wallpaper and better furniture. No one else could have spoken to him in such a fashion. But an old pastor's word back then was law.

So we went to church. Not frequently, not every Sunday, but enough to keep people from thinking we were heathens. When my parents did not go, we were transported to town so we could attend Sunday School. We went.

One did not work on Sunday. Exceptions were made only in harvest season with a snowstorm looming, or in haying weather, with the hay down and rain coming. Otherwise Sunday was for resting. The cows were milked and fed, eggs collected, a big Sunday lunch was prepared and duly eaten, but generally no other work was done. It was not a religious thing, with praying and churchly activity, but a day of rest. Usually my parents took a long Sunday afternoon nap and we had to be quiet. Willie and I were often in trouble on Sunday afternoons, since we did not nap, were bored, and, during bad weather, got into fights or arguments in the house. We did not rest.

Those childhood beliefs stick with a person. I do not understand how my children can attend church in their jeans. One should dress up for church. But I am equally guilty. I almost always work on Sunday, either at home or in the office.

The "day of rest" is gone. Actually, as I get older, I miss that. But I am still German in my attitude towards attending church. Once in a while is enough for my soul.

Kai Brost's confirmation.

Kai grew up in Oldenburg, Germany. He attended high school in Clarksville, Iowa, for a semester during his senior year, which left him with many funny insights regarding the American political process. He returned to Germany and graduated from an American high school on a nearby military base and then came back to Iowa, where he earned a degree from Wartburg College in Waverly, Iowa. He still keeps in contact with his high school friends from Germany and has a very close relationship with his grandmother, Hilda Fokkena.

One

By Heidi Sandler

When I was little (you were littler)
I pressed my nose to the glass,
Waiting for your six-hour journey
To end at our steps.
Hoped you were still awake
So we could braid our hair
And sing
And pretend to understand
Your dad and my mom.
So we could visit the park
That you gave a new name
And hunt for eggs
And (what else did we do?)

When I was older (not too much older)
You were the only one
Who thought I was cool.
I knew things
(or I thought I did)
like how to dry weed
kiss a boy
fall in love.
Or I pretended to
And you believed.
Your green eyes looking up at me
(can that be true?)
your small self in my clothes.

When you grew up
(you became the older one, you know)
you passed through my memories—
showed me how it's *really* done,
that falling in love stuff
and the rest, too.
And then I watched in awe
As you moved into yourself,
Three continents, two degrees
Your blonde hair Egyptian black.
But moreover claiming your words,
Your child,
As your own.

When I caught up,
We slowed our pace and moved through life
(our own and, again, each other's)
sometimes like adults
(work sleep eat work)
sometimes like children
(I *won't* go to sleep)
sometimes as one
(full circle, full table, secrets kept)
looking back
sometimes with wisdom
or (wine and) song
but never regret.

How It Is In Clarksville

By Rakaya El-Kasaby

I live in Boston. When I was younger I lived two hours away from Clarksville, in Iowa City. I started going to daycare there when I was four, so I would go to Clarksville on the weekends. My grandma came to my house, too. Now about what it was like in Clarksville.

I remember I would go in my mom's small green car. After about five minutes I realized the trip was very boring and would fall asleep. Occasionally I would have a pillow. When I got there it was dark. My mom would pull me up and I had fun ringing the doorbell or occasionally hiding away from the door and then jumping in. My mom would talk to Lisa and I sat on my grandma's lap. Then pretty soon my grandma would go to sleep and I enjoyed sleeping with her so I soon went to bed as well, after getting my nightly glass of water, of course. I went to sleep and I always seemed to wake up upside-down. It was weird, I don't do that anymore. Then in the morning I would wake up and my grandma would be up drinking coffee and she would get up and make some buttered toast, ask me if I would like some jam, and I would reply with a simple "no." She would cut off the crust and I would eat it. Then my grandma would get ready and I would play with my mom and Lisa's old toys or watch a movie. Then Grandma would dress me, walk me over to Oma's, though now I ride my scooter or my bike.

When I went to Oma's I would sit down and she would make me eggs for breakfast, and a hamburger or potatoes for lunch. Anything she makes is good. I never saw her burn anything. I would watch TV while eating and then I would go across the street and say hi to Aaron, Hannah, and Rachel. We would play and use Aaron's swingset. Then my grandma would pick me up at 4:30. Last time I was in Clarksville I stayed with Aaron and my grandma picked me up at Oma's. At the end of the day we would rent all these cool movies. I wanted my grandma to watch them with me but she stayed only for five minutes.

We are past sleeping so now about other things I do. Let's start with the store. The nearest store to me is Ken's. They have two cats there. At Ken's my grandma would buy me chocolate milk and candy. While I was waiting for Grandma, I would pet the cats. One of the cats was really shy so I didn't get to pet it. The other cat nudged my jacket and the man who works there said I had to leave my jacket there because that cat wanted it. (But he was just joking.) Other times I would go to the library. (I am guilty of leaving a book at Meta's for about two years, so could someone take it back please??) I would sometimes go down and listen as they read at storytime but sometimes I just get books. (Again, Mrs. Clark, I am really sorry about the book!)

Now about my Opa. I would go over to his office and use the computer. Sometimes he'd give me a Pepsi. Sometimes I would stay overnight at his house and play with Nala, his dog. Opa has lots of tractors and he mows the lawn a lot. Whenever I was doing any of these things, Grandma was usually working at the school. She has a hermit crab for a class pet. I hardly ever see its head out of its shell.

Now to compare. In Boston I can't walk anywhere by myself because of the traffic. I can do that in Clarksville though. The store near me in Boston is George's. It's got a cat, too. But personally, I like Ken's. In Boston, there are no farms like Opa's. (That means I can't have a dog!) All in all, I think Clarksville is better.

My Oma

By Katharina More

INTRODUCTION

I interviewed my grandma. Her name is Gerda Taylor. I interviewed her because I know a lot about her. I thought it would be a good idea if I chose her because then she could help me. I love her very much! And she loves me very much, too!

AS A YOUNG CHILD

My grandma lived in Germany. She went to school in the town of Walle. For fun, she played tag with the neighborhood kids. About 250 children went to her school. She did not like school at first. My grandma celebrated Easter, Christmas, Martin Luther Day, May Day, Mother's Day, and Father's Day. May Day and Martin Luther Day are different from today.

TEEN YEARS

Her favorite activities were meeting with friends and riding her bike. She went to a high school in Aurich. She had two hours' worth of homework, plus English. She wanted to be a flight attendant. Her friends were Gertrud, Ursel, Manfred, and Dieter. She had a job at a store.

AGE 20 to 30

She got married in the USA. She got married in June of 1965. She got married by the Justice of the Peace. She had two children. She did not have a job; she stayed at home and was a mother. Now she has lots of responsibility.

AGE OVER 30

Her life has changed since coming to the USA. She had to learn a new way to live in the USA and had to be away from her family. One sad story is she did not spend a lot of time with her mother. Her mother died when my grandma was in the USA.

A funny story is how she got words mixed up before she learned better English, like mushrooms & marshmallows. Mushrooms belong on pizza and marshmallows belong in a dessert, but once she ordered a pizza with marshmallows on it!

THE END

Reflection on a Journey

By Gerda Taylor

It was the summer of the year 1963 when I arrived in Chicago. My sponsor family, along with my cousin Meta, met me at O'Hare airport. We drove to Evanston, Illinois, where I took up residence in the home of these German friends.

I emigrated from the town of Aurich in northern Germany that May, and my first impressions of the United States were rather varied. I was totally impressed by the huge cars driven in America, the variety of people and nationalities one could meet, and the uncomplicated way of communication. I loved the way Americans showed interest in a "foreigner" and how eager they were to help. The German formality, which I was so used to but disliked so much, could be dropped.

But America was wrapped up in racial problems. Issues surrounding the "Negroes," as they were referred to back then, were on the news daily. Everyone was talking about the civil rights movement. Yes, these were the "turbulent 60s"! Martin Luther King, Jr. gathered groups together to march on Washington, D.C. to fight for the rights of Negroes. He gave a speech, demanding peace and equality.

I guess you could say I was facing some turbulence in my own life at that time. My English was pretty poor and I needed to find a job!

I had given up a very good job working for the government as court reporter and typist at the *Sozialgericht* (social security office) in Aurich, where formality in addressing one's superiors was of utmost importance. To enhance formality, we had to wear a *Talar* (a black robe) and a white starched blouse. The court hearings were held at the request of older people who, because of documents lost or burned in the war, needed to establish proof that indeed they had worked all their lives and were now eligible for Social Security. They had no proof of their age. Often a doctor, who was always present, would examine the person to find out their age and thereby establish eligibility for Social Security benefits.

Hilde, the wife of my German sponsor, mentioned that I should apply for a job at A.C. Nielsen in Chicago. She had worked there for several years and had liked it very much. I could take the number 2 bus down Ridge Avenue to Howard Street, she explained, and walk the rest of the way. But I thought I'd better try some other type of job—one that would be more forgiving of my struggling English skills. So I inquired at Wieboldts Department Store, which was located just across from where we lived. Unfortunately, there were no openings of any kind.

One morning I woke up with a terrible toothache, and my visit to the dentist became a blessing in disguise. Through broken English, using hands and feet, the dentist communicated to me that he desperately needed someone to watch his four children and to provide some help with household chores. His wife had recently passed away and there was no one to care for his children, the youngest being only four years old. I accepted eagerly—I now had my first job in the United States!

My employer provided me with a room in his beautiful Evanston home and paid me a good salary. I faced many challenges. I couldn't cook, and the modern American appliances were a mystery to me. Fortunately I had some experience with children and animals (the family owned a huge dog that was very fond of running away) and I knew how to clean house. Sarah, the four-year-old, warmed up to me very soon. She needed someone who could give her love and affection. Her sister Maggie, who was six years old, was very much interested in learning something about Germany. She would ask me to braid her long hair so that she would look like a German girl.

In the evening I would give the girls their bath and tried to "mother" them as much as possible. Unfortunately when it was time for bedtime stories, I discovered how little English I actually knew. But every night when I got halfway through one of Grimm's Fairy Tales, Sarah would say to me, "Don't worry, I will tell you the rest of the story." I was supposed to be teaching these kids, comforting them, caring for them. But at night, they became my teachers. During the year I spent with this family, I learned the English language of nursery rhymes, children's songs, and games. I am certain that I learned much more from the children than they learned from me. Their vacation home was in Luddington, Michigan, and after spending the summer there with them, the job ended. I took a boat back to Chicago, and somehow found my way back to Evanston where I once more occupied a room in the home of my friends.

I then took my friend Hilde's advice and began working in the office at A.C. Nielson, Marketing Research, in Chicago. It had a sort of international atmosphere. People from all over the world seemed to work there. I became friends with Barbro from Sweden, Betty from Holland, Delia from Peru, Elfriede and Helga from Germany, and Hannelore, who agreed to be my roommate.

Hannelore had been a model in Mannheim, Germany. Her family had lived in East Germany. It took them two weeks just to cross the border from East to West. In those days, the papers were full of stories about families escaping the harsh living conditions of East Germany under communist leadership. Many families took grave risks to flee the dictatorship for West Germany in order to have the freedom to settle and to live without fear. The Berlin Wall was adorned with wreaths and flowers in memory of those who were shot trying to cross the border. Hannelore was very grateful to now live in America.

She was not very interested in learning English; she was more interested in finding the "right boy" to marry. I needed to do the translating for her and her boyfriend. We worked full-time together at A.C. Nielsen, and I went to school at night. While I was studying English 100, I talked a lot to another student by the name of John. He seemed to feel sorry for me. I suppose I worked very hard in class in order to keep afloat with the American students. When John tried to whisper answers to me, the teacher would say, "Leave her alone—she can do this."

One Thursday evening after school, John and Ralph invited Hannelore and me to go out for pizza at a nearby restaurant. When it was time to order, I proudly proclaimed, "I would like pizza with marshmallows!" The waitress looked at me rather funny and asked me to repeat my order. "Put marshmallows on my pizza, please," I insisted. The conversation went back and forth—she even asked in the kitchen about pizza with marshmallows—until my friend recommended I draw a picture of a marshmallow. That gave it away—I drew a perfect picture of a mushroom!

A year later, I left A.C. Nielsen and found a position at a company near the Merchandise Mart in downtown Chicago. Now I needed to take the "El" train to work every day and got a closer, not-very-attractive look at the city of Chicago. On the long, over-crowded ride to work I often wondered why people would choose to live in a big city such as Chicago. The view from the "El" was of old and run-down homes, where gray laundry hung out to dry between even grayer buildings. The buildings were so close together that it had to be hard to breathe, I thought. I had never lived in an apartment before—this was my first!

I was glad that I didn't live alone in my apartment. I was also glad that my roommate was German. We had countless discussions about the United States versus Germany. As months went by, we realized more and more how much the USA differed from the old country. Hannelore was still anxious to follow her dream, and that dream was to meet the man she would marry. She didn't have to wait very long. At the wedding reception held for our friends Betty and Alfredo, Hannelore met someone from Texas and she soon began to make her own wedding pans.

It was springtime in 1965 when I was introduced to someone by the name of Mike Sandler. Mike's friend Norman thought that we would make an interesting couple and arranged a blind date. Mike and I met, went to dinner that night, and took a long walk exploring the neighborhood. We talked for what seemed like forever, and that night we fell in love. There was something special about the way Mike talked to me and the questions he asked about my upbringing in Germany. I felt that he was a caring man who was smart and confident in his planning for the future.

Several weeks of fun and getting to know one another went by when Mike suddenly became interested in talking about religion. He wondered whether I knew what his religion was! It had not occurred to me that his beliefs could differ greatly from mine. And so I guessed every religion I could possibly think of, but I was wrong every time! Finally, he said, "I am Jewish."

I looked at my roommate and she looked back at me. *"Was ist 'Jewish'?"* We reached for the German-American dictionary and found Jewish. *Juedisch.* A Jew was a *Jude.* Mike was *ein Jude*—the first Jew I had ever met, and I was madly in love with him! How incredibly strange that I should fall in love with the first Jewish person I had ever met in my life!

After some sleepless nights, a lot of soul searching and many long walks, I decided to write to my mother's sister, my aunt, who lived in Iowa. She called me right away and told me how upset she was, and that I needed to write and explain the situation to my mother in Germany. But the more I thought of ending the relationship, the more I decided I couldn't do it. I knew I loved Mike—there was no getting around it. My worries escalated when Mike told his parents about me and about his wish to get married. His parents advised him to finish his college education and then meet a nice Jewish girl—and to stay away from "Gentiles."

Mike and I knew that we would be terribly unhappy, but we tried to end the relationship. We promised not to call each other. I did a lot of thinking about the war and what atrocities and crimes the Germans had committed, especially towards the Jews. I was a child raised in post-war Germany, and I couldn't help but wonder what kind of feelings Mike's family might have toward Germans. Programs about the Second World War and the unbelievable numbers of Jews killed in concentration camps were still viewed by many in America. I had very little education on the subject—German schools didn't yet teach their students that part of German history. I had to learn about it from books and from others.

My friends would sometimes invite me to parties. On one of those Saturday evenings, I met a German man named Klaus. We talked and he explained that he had come to the States to get an education in medicine. We liked each other and talked a lot about Germany, especially about the town Hamburg where his family lived. He asked if I would take a trip with him to Germany to meet his family.

I began thinking that maybe it was time to go back to Germany together with Klaus. Maybe I, too, had gotten something of an education here, but maybe my place was in Germany, back with my own family. Whenever I was in the company of Klaus, however, I missed Mike terribly. I knew that Mike had dropped out of school—he just couldn't concentrate on his studies. He simply had too much on his mind.

After some time had passed, Mike came to see me. He brought flowers, the way it is done in Germany, and said that we should talk. He asked that I forget everything that had been bothering me and marry him. He claimed that he didn't care what his parents thought; our love for each other was all that mattered to him. I told him that I needed a weekend to think about this and promised him that I would make a decision one way or the other.

So I took a train and bus to visit a long-time German friend, Gertrud, who lived on the south side of Chicago. Her husband was a professional soldier and had been transferred to Chicago. She was alone with her little girl.

We spent an entire day discussing my future—Mike versus Klaus, USA versus Germany—and Gertrud and I agreed that since I loved Mike, the answer was really very simple. I would stay and marry him.

I called Mike that very evening. He came to pick me up as soon as he could, and when I heard the sound of his old Volkswagen—a sound which had become very dear to me—through the open windows, I ran down four flights of stairs to the parking lot and into his arms. Tears rolled down our faces when we spoke of marriage and having babies.

We eloped and were married by a Justice of the Peace on June 25, 1965.

Recovery

By Heidi Sandler

It was early January, the disco was full, and I had just spent the past several days in bed with the worst cold I had ever had. This cold was the result of our previous trip to the disco, the week before, New Year's Eve 1993-94. We couldn't get a taxi home to my uncle's farm in rural Aurich, Germany, and we ended up walking the whole way. It sounds like the kind of thing that happened to teenagers, but I was twenty-five and recently divorced.

I was in Johnny's Dancing Disco (who named this place?), which everyone called Dieling's, presumably because that was Johnny's last name. I was with my only male cousins, Gerrit and Onno. While their primary motive was the pursuit of alcohol, mine was dancing, something I rarely did anymore in the States. Gerrit never danced—I had never once seen him dance—but Onno was willing to dance with me occasionally and that was all that mattered. And was it FUN! Dieling's played all the best music, and Tony the DJ remembered me when I visited from Chicago. In fact, he played songs *by* Chicago in my honor, and I felt important for three minutes, forty-eight seconds.

I had been to Aurich about seven times in my life. My mother's brother and his family owned a dairy farm here, in northern Niedersachsen (Lower Saxony), about an hour-and-a-half from the Dutch border. I loved it here. I loved the openness that I never saw in the suburbs. I loved the animals that I knew nothing about. I loved the customs, the rich and harsh languages, the mild weather. When I was sixteen I wanted to live here. When I was twenty-three, I did live here. This place, this country, this *town* had a hazy, mysterious atmosphere that was unlike the feeling I got from any other vacation spot. Maybe because this was more than a vacation. This was my family, this was my home, too.

My mother was born in Germany; she learned to walk here, fell down, fell in love, and, like any proper young woman, yearned to leave her hometown. These people (who either spoke my native language with beautiful accents or not at all) had my blood running through them. Their DNA strings had *something* of mine in them. I was part of this place, this town, this disco.

My mother did leave, though, at age twenty-four; she went as far as she figured she could go and still be forgiven for leaving. She went to Chicago, married my Jewish father (was forgiven for that, too), and had me and my brother. We visited Germany every two or three years from the time I was twelve. After that, we traveled to Aurich whenever we could afford it or decided it was "necessary."

Because it was deemed "necessary" for my mother to travel to Germany in December of 1993 to deal with some legal papers concerning my grandmother's property, and because it was further necessary that I travel with my mother to guide her through the airports and to drive her from Point A (Amsterdam) to Point A-prime (Aurich) in a stick-shift rental car that she couldn't drive if her life depended on it (did I mention that the woman grew *up* here in the land of Volkswagen We-Don't-Even-Make-Automatic-Transmissions-In-This-Country Beetles?), here I was in Johnny's Dancing Disco with my male cousins.

And in walked Frank.

When I came here for my twelfth birthday, I met a few of my cousin Gerrit's friends. The two that hung around most often were Willi and Frank. I remember we tossed a ball around in the front yard of the farm house, trying to hit each other with it as hard as possible. We played soccer in the side yard, near the beehives that my uncle kept (we later called the farm "The Land of Milk and Honey"), my cousin Onno fiercely guarding the goal. I remember most clearly, though, that Willi, Frank, and Gerrit spun me on the tire swing in the hayloft, around and around until I nearly threw up from dizziness—that, of course, being their goal.

At age twelve I was interested in all boys, friends of my cousins included. I waited each day for them to show up, and when my cousin bounded outside to roughhouse or start up a game, I was right behind him, tagging along like a younger sister, though I was a year older. Chasing the boys within the proper confines of a game of chase. That's how I spent my six weeks in my personal heaven.

Throughout the years, I saw Frank occasionally at parties, or in the discos, always glad to greet him with a hug, and try out my faltering German on him (he never learned more than a few words of English), but I never had any idea he was at all interested in me during those adolescent years. Perhaps he never was. But when he walked into a full Dieling's Disco that night in early January, as I was getting over my cold, his adolescence had been replaced with confidence and very grown-up good looks.

Frank was not tall, but he was muscular, with broad shoulders and strong-looking hands. He had short, sandy-blonde hair and a quick, sweet smile. His eyes noticed everything and they crinkled when he laughed.

He had learned no more English since I had seen him last, but by then my German was good enough to carry me. We talked first of simple things: did I want a drink, a cigarette? (No, and yes, several.) How long was I in town? Where was my daughter? With my answers came the piece of information that he had been looking for: I was in town with my mother, and there was no one back home who could claim me.

The next thing he told me is something I will remember forever; a sentence I still replay in my mind when I feel under-confident or unattractive: *"I've wanted to kiss you for fourteen years."*

There is something to be said (I'm not sure what, but *something*, something really meaningful and important, something that every young woman should carry with her) for being told, in the foreign language you have loved all your life, by a handsome European man, that he has been waiting for the last fourteen years to kiss you. As if his life couldn't be complete until he had done just that. As if then and only then, could he die happy.

I wish I could remember the exact German phrasing he used, but I can't. It wouldn't be the same, anyway, not without his Ostfriesen accent and gravelly voice. What I remember is the idea that this guy had been thinking about me, wondering, anticipating this moment for a long time, even though I was rarely in the same town, rarely on the same continent. That during odd moments in his otherwise full life, my face filled his mind. My face. *Me.* A girl he had seen a handful of times; a regular, average girl from the other side of the world. From my place in that world, age twenty-five and starting over already, this idea amazed and thrilled me.

These are the moments that keep us going. For some reason, the memory of this moment fills me with confidence, energy, tenderness, whatever it is I am lacking and desperately need at the time.

And these moments are such small, inconsequential ones, really, when you take the long view. Of all the men in my life, before him and since, Frank is the one I spent the least time with. He was a small part of my life; I was certainly an even smaller part of his. But these are the parts we keep.

"I've wanted to kiss you for fourteen years."

I wonder if he caught my cold.

Bad Zwischenahn is located just south of Aurich in Ammerland. Hanni Fecht sent this post card to her granddaughter, Heidi, while Heidi was attending Northern Illinois University.

In the Middle Ages the area around Bad Zwischenahn was considered a buffer zone against the unpredictable Frisians. The St. Johannes Church was built there in 1124. Prior to World War II the town was home to a civil airport, but it was taken over by the Luftwaffe in 1939. It sustained damage from several bombing campaigns between 1944 and 1945 before it was captured by Canadian forces in April of 1945. It is a now a resort town famous for its spas.

Above: Phil and Heidi Sandler, Gesa and Onno Fecht. Rahe, summer 1972.
Below: Gerrit Fecht, Rahe. Christmas, 1972.

Once and Again

By Heidi Sandler

It is now another early January, 2002, and I have just returned home from my tenth visit to Ostfriesland. This time I traveled not only with my mother, but with my two daughters, ten-year-old Katharina and six-year-old Joelle. The four of us spent Christmas and New Year's in the apartment house my grandmother owned and lived in before she died.

The first sensation I remember feeling about this particular trip was how strange it was going to be to visit this country without Oma Hanni's presence. I felt that strangeness in the anticipation of the trip, and I felt it as we drove from Schiphol Airport into Germany. Yes, from Point A (Amsterdam) to Point A-prime (Aurich), in a stick shift rental car my mother still couldn't drive. Yes, we're home.

The bottom apartment of the building was rented to strangers, and the peculiar feeling became ever stronger as we took a brief tour of the rooms Oma Hanni had lived in when she was alive. Joelle had never met Oma Hanni, and this saddened me in a way I could never—will never—shake. I could never change this fact; I could never make this right.

An even stronger sensation for me, however, was the need to see and feel Germany through my children. I had been coming to Aurich regularly since I was three. I had been there with my family, with a college friend, with my husband and child, and by myself. I had been nursed back to health there, learned to drive stick shift there (how ironic is that?), had fallen in love there. I was connected, and desperately wanted my children to feel the connection just as deeply.

Katie had lived in Germany for three months as an infant and had visited in 1998, but Joelle had never been in this town—a notion I found almost ridiculous. How could a child of mine be six years old and never have set foot on this piece of the earth? Yet she was seeing this place for the first time, and I wanted to absorb every minute of it with her—with both of them...every nuance they noticed, every emotion they experienced.

There are a lot of things that I have passed down to my children, outside of physical appearance—things that I'm proud to claim as something "she got from me." Joelle's fascination with words, Katie's interest in brain teasers, their love of music and musicals. I wanted my perpetual sense of awe of this country to instill itself in them as well. I wanted it to settle into their very bones, along with a feeling of true belonging—in this place, this country, this town.

But children don't take anything for granted. To them, nothing is a given. To a child, climbing up steps for the first time, or learning to ride a two-wheeler, or walking to the park alone with a girlfriend is The Greatest Show On Earth. If the thrill of Disney World can't compare, if the Grand Canyon can't compare, at least not yet, when the whole world is a marvelous jumble of newness, how then can I expect the airport, the strange new Euro coins, the beautiful scenery on the way to a foreign village to capture their hearts?

Although the weather in Ostfriesland that winter was uncharacteristically snowy and icy and cold, and although we got lost at least twice on the way into Germany, Katie and Joey were happy to be in Aurich. They bundled up and explored the brightly-colored *Weihnachtsmarkt* as soon as we arrived, excited to be Christmas shopping for their Oma and each other in an atmosphere further from Woodfield Mall than they could imagine.

They were overjoyed to finally meet their two-year-old cousin Ilva, whom they fawned over constantly, and who rewarded them with wide-eyed attention and even an attempt at cross-cultural communication.

And Katie and Joey settled easily into the routine of the day: rising to wash in the bedroom's basin, quickly dressing near the radiator before the cold of the house caught up, eating the almost-familiar meals with the almost-familiar rumbling of *Plattdeutsch* discussion echoing around them.

My heart was quietly pleased to finally sit with my daughters in the Eiscafe, or the Pinocchio restaurant, or Tante Riki's kitchen, the kitchen that was the heart not only of the farmhouse, but of my adolescent memories. If I could bring my children there, if I could walk with them on the *Fußgängerzone*, if I could photograph them in the places whose images were burned into my heart, then I could somehow find a way to make them understand the draw of this land. And I could give that to them.

In the end, they truly enjoyed it. That's really the strongest word I can use, at least until the next trip. They loved the farm, the people, the food, the things they brought home. They enjoyed, I'm thankful to say, using the language of their family.

But were they touched by the country itself? By this place, this town that, even to this day, keeps me awake the night before a trip, rushed with the adrenaline of anticipation? I can't say they were in awe; I can't say they loved it. But this was their family; this was their home, too, and they felt the common roots. The seeds were planted.

◆   ◆   ◆

Every once in a while, my senses will betray me. I'll walk into Rosk-a-Deli for lunch, near my office in northern Illinois, and the strong, pleasant scents will pull me back to Tante Riki's kitchen. Or the Chicago weather will suddenly be just the right sort of mild and peaceful, and I'll just *feel* Germany.

One recent evening, months after our return, the three of us sat at the dinner table. Katie, who had picked up Gerrit's habit of putting ketchup on everything, mixed up her potatoes on her plate, Aurich-style, and took a bite.

"Yum, this is how Germany tastes!"

My heart fluttered as I turned to her and saw myself. I smiled and I heard the "click." The connection has been made.

We've come full circle.

All About Germany

By Joelle Kasprisin (written in 2002)

I only went to Germany once.
It was very nice there.
I played with my sister Katie and my cousin Ilva.
It was snowing a lot.
The snow was about six inches high.
We had Christmas in Germany.
I got a lot of presents.
Ilva, Katie, and I put the ornaments on the Christmas tree.
The Christmas tree was real!
My Uncle Garrelt was brave enough to go into the woods to chop the tree down!
On New Year's Eve, we went to Ilva's mother Gesa's house for dinner.
Then we watched fireworks!
I loved it there.
It was the best trip ever!

Joelle Kasprisin, Rahe, Germany. Christmas, 2001.

Torn Between Open Spaces

By Gunda J. Brost

I'm seven.

LaGuardia airport in New York City. This is my first time in America, let alone in any very different place. And this is a different type of place. The hustle and bustle of people hurrying to some unknown destination heaves a rush over the endlessly huge hall covered with windows that extend to the sky. I look around me. Africans in colorful garb, patterns all wild and dizzy, their faces expressive and kind as they speak and gesture with each other. Asians in understated dark blue suits, very serious expressions on their faces. The Indian women wear a mark on their forehead, glistening in the changing light. Their silky, soft garments flow airily around their bodies as they move, delightfully bright colors bringing out the soft brown tone of their skin. Shining gold is everywhere, on their necks, hands, fingers, even on their toes. And Arab families, men leading, women following, the children holding their mother's hands. Veils cover the women's faces, but their intense, mysterious eyes dominate their presence. I stare and stare and stare. The music of many different languages drifts over me. I try to pick out words but the meanings of their sounds elude me. Thankfully, people in such a place are too busy to have time to mind the intrusive curiosity of a wide-eyed girl who can only stare at them.

Outside, it is pouring. My mother grabs the children, my father grabs the luggage, and we all head to a taxi stand. The cab driver is a broad-shouldered black man. He and my dad yell at each other. There's honking, louder than any traffic I have ever heard. The darkness of night is torn apart by the aggressive in-your-face neon lights. We are in America. I am terrified and fascinated. My father is angry and strong and protective. I feel scared and safe at the same time.

I'm twelve.

My mother comes home with new clothes for me and lays them out on my bed to show me. I am surprised. My mother has never bought me this many nice clothes before. There is a sheer white blouse, with tiny flower-shaped holes in it.

107

There are shiny blue leather shoes with an elegant heel. I have never worn high heels before. There is a dress, long; red, white, and blue. I have never worn a dress other than when I played dress-up or when I snuck up into my mom's room to try on her wedding dress when she was gone. There are three pairs of bras, two white and one beige. I have never worn a bra before. This is the first time I am made aware of my budding breasts. I feel proud, proud that I am female. My mother talks non-stop. She is excited. *You're going to America. You will meet your aunties and your cousins. Remember when you met them when you were seven?* I remember. My aunties were loud and friendly and constantly petting my head. They always called me "honey" and "sweetheart." My mom was not going to come along on this trip. I could tell she had tears in her eyes.

A few days short of the flight, nature interfered. I got my period for the first time. I didn't know what was happening to me. I thought I had some deadly disease, that my insides were bleeding. I had been in the hospital once when I was seven, and the doctors never did figure out what had been wrong with me that time. Maybe whatever it was had now come back? My mom said no, that I didn't have a disease. She said it in a way that I believed her. She gave me the instructions of a tampon box, but didn't say much else. I was very confused.

On the airplane my brother and I drank all the soda we could stomach. We had grown up in a household in which sugar was carefully monitored. All of a sudden we could finish a drink of Seven Up or ginger ale and just ask the friendly stewardess for another one, and it would be immediately forthcoming. No questions, no comments, only friendly smiles and a "here you are." No limits.

We arrived at my dad's family reunion. My aunties were all there, so different from my mother. My mother wore very simple clothes and put her long hair up into a bun. She never wore any makeup, except maybe brow liner. My aunties had big, curly, colorful hair and extravagant clothes. Their nails were long and round and hard and glittered like snowy mountaintops. They wore big, heavy rings whose weight pulled on their fingers. They were outspoken and humorous. Their voices were loud and friendly. They teased me and each other a lot. They sipped exotic long drinks and smoked Virginia Slims. They played cards. They always called me "sweetie" or "honey." I adored my aunties.

Midway through the vacation my period came and never left. I think I had my period for several weeks, almost the entire trip. I couldn't talk to my dad about this. I couldn't talk to my brother about this. My mother and sister were back home in Germany. Finally, I assume, my cousins figured out what was going on and filled my dad in. I had to swallow some awful-tasting medicine that was supposed to balance my hormones. My dad still never broached the subject with me.

I was very tall for my age. Nobody believed that I was twelve. When we went on amusement park rides or to museums the signs would say: "Children under thirteen, half-price." I was embarrassed when my dad would argue that I was twelve and he should only have to pay half-price for me. I wanted people to think I was older because I didn't want them to think, "Oh my God, she is twelve? But she is sooo tall!" My dad didn't understand why I was arguing with him. He thought I was just being difficult.

I was twelve and in a foreign country and becoming a woman, whether I wanted to or not, but nobody could explain what that meant to me. I felt very lonely.

My dad gave most of his attention during the trip to my little brother. But one evening as we were walking home from some concert I slipped next to him and put my arm in his and walked home arm in arm with him. It seemed to make him feel awkward, though. My heart ached. I thought back to La Guardia and wished for the dad I'd had at that time, strong and sure of himself and guiding me along.

I tasted adventure that summer. I saw wagon tracks made by people who risked their lives to cross the country. I thought if they weren't scared, why should I be? I saw Independence Rock, where the hopeful had immortalized their names and little comments into the neutral, receptive witness of stony indefiniteness. Reflections of their broken dreams remain to remind passers-by to take charge of life. I set my feet on virgin land: it felt like few people had walked this way before. I searched wide open spaces for never-ending horizons. I came as close as I have ever been to the real bears that approached our car as we slowly drove by. I experienced the ghost towns of the West, which sprinkled the vast empty land, haunted by desperate nothingness, abandoned for the endless human quest to seize happiness, that elusive concept. In their dust, they left their legacy, the irony of their quest: in attempting to make history, most of them never did, at least not as individuals, but their collective stories forever tantalize our imagination for their sheer triviality, like Pompeii.

I'm seventeen.

I am sort of an exchange student. I live with my aunt and uncle and cousin in a small, rural community in Iowa. At school everyone seems so much alike. All the boys wear athletic gear, tennis shoes, and have short hair. In Germany there were more groups. My clothes are different. Nobody takes school seriously. In Germany if you didn't take school seriously you would end up on the street.

I miss the German individuality.

I attract attention.

For the first time in my life, boys tell me I am beautiful. But neither they nor the girls seem to want to be friends with me. Like an exotic caged animal attraction at the zoo, I can only reach out for the shallowness of this attention to fill my loneliness.

I'm nineteen.

I am back in America. I have convinced my parents to let me come study here because I love America. People are so much friendlier there, and there are so many opportunities to study at an American college. In Germany at my age you have to know what you want to do with the rest of your life or you can forget about your future. I do not know what I want to do with my life yet. My life has just begun! I can't decide, out of all those wonderful subjects, which one I'm most interested in. Since my grades are fantastic, and because my parents sense that I have many little talents but none to dominate the direction my life will take, they agree.

I live a somewhat wild life. I'm very involved politically. The international students are my substitute family. But sometimes cultures clash. I am driven by an unidentified, restless force. Experiencing alcohol, and sex. But they never satisfy the deep longing in me. I have a hole in my soul.

I'm thirty-two.

I am in law school. German acquaintances raise their eyebrows: How can you go back to school with a little child? Aren't you too old to start a whole new career? It is useless to try to explain to them. I have become Americanized: I am a pioneer. Nothing is impossible; you just have to keep looking for new solutions and face problems head-on. I have the drive and energy and focus.

I look at my son, asleep. The complete peacefulness, innocence, and abandon of my sleeping child grounds me. It helps me focus on what is really important in this life.

My grandparents came to this country as real immigrants. They spent their entire lives torn between the two cultures they loved. They would live here for a while and then there for a while. It seems they never felt complete happiness. It is the legacy of my blood to be restless. My grandma is eighty-seven and still wants to "retire" in Germany! This force and drive has annoyed me countless times. But it also makes me who I am.

Sometimes, the wide open spaces are inhabited by those with closed minds. And sometimes, the next-door anonymity of living in a complex tightly-spaced big city makes you open your mind as wide as horizons of the American West.

As for me, I am torn between open spaces, looking for a cultural identity to cling to. I have no real home or culture; I have several. I hope my son will be the link. He is the real American. He was born in this country. Yet people looking at our skin colors would assume I am the "American" and he is more likely to be the "foreigner." My son will have to struggle with three cultural influences: African, American, and European. But I have confidence in him: when I was still pregnant, I named him my "prince of peace" because I was so happy he was coming. And indeed he is a prince of peace in that the happiness he has shown me made me forgive myself and others many shortcomings. My hope is that he will be able to synthesize all his uniqueness and simply be himself, grounded and at home.

Maybe this is what it really means to be a true American.

Auf'm Bahnhof Zoo im Damenklo

By Laura Fokkena

Berlin, 1991

I've come to Germany with Kurt. He's one of my oldest friends; we grew up together in Clarksville. He's been suave since childhood and he's suave today, smoking a cigarette and looking bored in the middle of Berlin's central train station, appropriately called the Zoo. It's a madhouse, 10 o'clock at night and riddled with an all-too-perfect cross-section of the kind of population that makes Berlin a kind of mystical Shangri-La for American punks dreaming of escape from their suburban Minneapolis homes. I dump my backpack with Kurt and leave him among the freaks to hunt for a bathroom.

The one I find takes me downstairs a flight of stairs, but my passage is blocked halfway by a dead woman. She's my age but beautiful, artistically spread across ten or twelve steps, her make-up still perfect: dark brown lipstick expertly applied, her hair dyed burgundy and cropped around her chin, her cheeks bleached with that air-brushed quality that only the dead can achieve. I am mesmerized. Should I call the police, I wonder? An ambulance?

At the foot of the steps stands an elderly woman with gray hair, a smart apron and arms angrily akimbo, looking so Old-World-matronly that I wonder if she got lost in the Zoo on her way to Ostfriesland. But then I realize she must work here; maybe she is some kind of cleaning woman, perhaps the restroom monitor. (Does the Zoo have such things?)

I ask if a doctor has been called, and she snarls at me. I frown in confusion. My question seemed pretty innocuous, even obvious. But maybe I made a mistake in German and have been misunderstood. It wouldn't be the first time. For years I would say *"ich bin heiss"*—"I am hot"—on the rare occasion when the temperature in northern Germany topped seventy degrees, all the while being unaware that the correct phrase was *"mir ist heiss,"* and that *"ich bin heiss"* also means "I am hot" but carries a sexual connotation. Only after hearing this double innuendo explored in the lyrics of a Nina Hagen song did this linguistic phenomenon become clear to me, and by then it was too late. I'd already informed hundreds of Germans, including great-uncles and my friends' employers, that *oh* I was *so hot.*

"*Drogen,*" she says with a sneer. *Drugs.* She studies the dead girl with disgust, as I study the violet bruises on the underside of the poor girl's elbow. The old woman understood me perfectly well. She just didn't see the need to go chasing after help, breaking a sweat, no doubt, when this girl had clearly Broken The Rules. If she was going to mess around with heroin it was her own damn fault she was lying there now, *nicht?*

And now I am doubly fascinated. How is it, I wonder, that she can muster righteous indignation even in an obvious emergency? I'd like to have been surprised. I'd like to chalk it up to the insensitivity of this *particular* old woman, but if there's one thing my German background is full of it's old women, and if there's one emotion with which I am acutely familiar it's righteous indignation.

American movies like to pretend that moral outrage is the prerogative of age. How else do you explain Ronald Reagan? But when you actually hang out with old women in the United States you get a completely different picture. When I was in teenager I spent a good portion of my time writing articles for the school newspaper about abortions, AIDS, drug use, alcoholism, pornographic rock music and the pros and cons of showing condom ads on television. The mothers of other students dutifully complained to the appropriate school officials, but the older women—"the little old ladies" as my father called them—appeared at his office with compliments. "Gets people thinking!" they told him with delight.

Not so in Germany. German grandmothers are the arbiters of morality and good sense. There are exceptions, of course, but my own Oma wasn't one of them. She had tales upon tales of the downfalls that befell young women who never learned to cook, who experimented with illegal substances, who flirted too much, who played tennis instead of keeping their husbands happy.

And I knew this.

I knew this in 1987 when I fell hopelessly in love with a young German boy named Willi. He was a friend of my cousin; we found each other in the midst of smoke and pounding Cure music in a German discothek in the middle of the night. This was in the days before e-mail, so after I left in August we wrote to each other the old-fashioned way, with pens and pencils, like lovers in a war. I spent the next five months convincing my parents that spending a semester going to a German school would make me well-rounded and culturally aware. They bought it.

It was raining (of course) when I returned in February. What had once been the overcast land of my ancestors had suddenly transformed itself into a romantic European adventure; every broken cobblestone was now erupting with possibilities. I'd spent the previous five months waking up from dreams that I was *there*, that he was only a bike ride away. And now he was. My grandparents were vaguely aware of my "crush," but they cataloged it under the romanticism of youth. This misunderstanding would color the rest of my trip.

A German teacher and friend of the family had offered me a place to stay during that semester. Despite the fact that he had a tap installed in his home and served my underage self a mammoth stein of Beck's Dark at dinner the one time I ate with his family, I decided to stay with my grandparents, thinking that my familiarity with them would make my life easier. And in many ways it did. My Oma is perhaps the only person out there who loves me so unconditionally, who sacrifices so much for me with so few expectations of any return on her investment. She took on the task of caring for me with a vengeance, a ferocious sense of protection that my own parents had never had the tenacity to adopt, even if they agreed with it in principle. Oma studied Willi, viewing him as a potential husband for me, a prospect that took me, a sophomore in high school, very much by surprise.

In the beginning she liked him. For in Ostfriesland there are two kinds of young men: those who accept Ostfriesland for what it is and those who long to escape. The latter were called "poppers" and frequented the posh restaurants and discos (or what passed for posh in Aurich), separating themselves from the farm boys and speaking only High German, even if they understood *Plattdeutsch* perfectly well.

Willi was not in this category. He spoke Low German like my father, harsh and abrupt, allowing two syllables for words like "ja" *("yo-ah")*, and took great interest in all things mechanical. When you poured his tea he did not murmur *no, stop, thank you, that's enough*, like the pretentious popper boys, but rather threw up a calloused hand and cried "Ho!" just like my Opa. This my Oma approved of. Willi was one of us. If we married, she assured us, she'd give us eighty acres of farmland in Iowa. What we would do with it was unclear, but it was ours for the taking.

But her opinion slowly soured. The more I escaped into the world of Willi, the more she panicked. Were things getting too serious? I was fifteen, after all, and Willi was nineteen, an adult, really.

And when an Oma panics, she does not do it alone. No, she gets on the phone and calls every last trusted acquaintance—that is, all twenty-four family members living within a 200-kilometer radius—and asks them for their opinion on her plight. Thus if I missed my curfew by half an hour I could be very much assured that twenty-four relatives in northern Germany would be aware of my absence before I even made it home.

Occasionally, in a moment of bravery, she would actually call America and ask my father for his opinion on this relationship. He hemmed and hawed and tried to appease everyone, caring little for what was happening 4,000 miles away. Nevertheless, she took him on as her proxy, convinced that he shared her own view on this and every other issue, a belief of hers that to this day keeps my dad from telling her that he eats out at restaurants several times a week—a waste of money she would find inexcusable.

How much of her attitude was the result of her own values and how much was worry over what other people would think if she let me run awry was uncertain. In fact I'm not sure such a distinction even existed. My mother, for example, struggles with what she thinks is right and what she thinks she has to do so people won't say nasty things about her. Often she finds herself going against her own code of ethics or pretending to care about things she thinks are irrelevant just to appease strangers, and then resenting herself for it. I do the same.

But I don't think Oma has this problem. What's right *is* what keeps other people from talking; avoiding gossip is the very definition of living correctly. Hence her opposition to the fact that I wore ripped jeans wasn't born of worry that I'd get cold knees—it was (and she admitted this to me) her terror over the thought that a woman she'd gone to confirmation classes with fifty years earlier would see me riding down the street on my bicycle and think that Oma was either too destitute to buy me respectable pants, or too lazy to sew patches on the ones I had. Ergo I would wear uncomfortable slacks as I rode past that woman's house and change into my well-worn jeans once I got to school. This solution satisfied us both.

But, unfortunately for Oma, there is no talking to a fifteen-year-old in love for the first time, especially a fifteen-year-old in the midst of a foreign romance with someone who's written her *actual love letters* for half a year. Her crusade was lost from the day my plane landed.

But was she a quitter? Oh no. This is a woman who'd nearly given birth in a bomb shelter, a woman who showed up at my apartment at the age of seventy-six and crawled across my hardwood floors with a wet paper towel, scrubbing years of caked-on dust off the baseboards, all the while whispering, *"Really, Laury, you should have done this yourself."* Oma is nothing if not tenacious.

The holes in the jeans were one thing, but being seen all over Ostfriesland in the company of a boy? Maybe if all the neighbors and relatives had known me my whole life, seen me grow up, knew that I did well in school, counted on me to watch their kids now and then, maybe then it wouldn't have mattered so much. At my Tante Riki's, for instance, they'd all known Willi longer than they'd known me; he practically grew up on their farm, helped with the hay, and could identify the cows by their individual personalities. His little brother still helps them make *Silo* each spring. There he and I were like the barn and the bicycles and the work boots piled outside their door: just part of the scenery. But outside that refuge I was nothing but a typical teenager, flaky (read: American) to the core, and suffering from a serious case of mixed-up priorities. It was up to Oma to straighten me out.

Clearly, our relationship was changing.

No longer a pre-schooler under her featherbed, I was no longer a candidate for lenience, for tolerance, for exemption from the expectations she had of everyone else. I was growing up. My whims were no longer indulged. I did not appreciate this changing climate. Not at all.

Over breakfast of Müsli and tea, she entertains me with a story about the neighbor woman whose daughter had to fly to England for an abortion.

"Why are you telling me this?"

"Tja," she answers simply, sucking in her breath and returning to the dishes. My Opa can be heard stirring in the next room. Soon he will come in, wearing his sturdy brown pants and plain, practical suspenders, wanting breakfast before he takes his bicycle out for his morning ride. The conversation—what there was of it—comes to a halt. Some things cannot be said in front of men. This censorship stems not from her embarrassment over sex, but her belief that the world is divided into separate spheres. There is the men's world, which is filled with work and warfare, and the women's world, the world of food and whispered conversations, and a great deal of blood: from childbirth, from menstruation, from virginity lost, from the bumps and bruises of children falling from trees and rooftops even after you *told* them not to climb so high. Blood can be washed out of linens with cold water. Men needn't be bothered with how it got there.

And secrets. The women's world is full of secrets. Cheating husbands, disloyal siblings, families fractured by arguments over inheritance and property back when there was precious little inheritance or property to argue over. Such stories are told only in times of stress, for they have a very specific purpose: *do you want to add your name to this genre of family folklore?* Ok, then. *Whatever it is you're doing, knock it off.* I was finally old enough to be initiated into this circle of shrouded tales, with their serious, moralistic themes and frightening endings. (Is it any wonder that the Brothers Grimm, authors of legends that involved children being abandoned by their parents and eaten by wolves, were German?) My new-found maturity was a mixed blessing, to be sure.

If Oma lived for what the neighbors thought, my Opa lived for what my Oma thought. He rarely offered opinions on any issue, controversial or otherwise, but he had a precise awareness of when Oma had reached her limit. One evening the three of us were watching a TV show about nuclear war. I was rarely able to follow German television, but the grim sight of a girl with matted hair crawling out of a bomb shelter, tongue hanging out, crying for her family, needed no linguistic clarification. I had a train wreck fascination with the program, but after the second or third time Oma complained about the sick tragedy unfolding in our living room, Opa turned to me sharply and shouted, *"das ist genug!"—that's enough!* He snapped off the television and told me to find myself something to read.

Geez, I didn't write the show, I grumbled to myself, though I knew better than to protest out loud. Still, even at the time, I was impressed with him. I could do what I liked with the rest of my life, but taxing Oma's emotions was strictly off-limits. That was his singular rule, his sole guiding principle, and the fact that he was silent about so many things made this one commandment all the more powerful whenever it materialized.

Given the threat I posed to her blood pressure and mental health, I sometimes wonder why Oma took me in at all. At the time it was something I took so much for granted that it hardly merited comment, but the more I observe extended families in the United States, the more surprising it is that Oma is, well, Oma.

My daughter has a storybook about a (presumably American) grandmother who travels to the jungle, the Arctic, up and down the Nile, always returning with gifts for her granddaughter. She loves her granddaughter more than she loves her adventures (of course—otherwise the book would hardly be marketable to children), but that love doesn't keep her at home in a rocker, knitting quilts. No, this grandma is always pictured with a pair of binoculars, trailing bulky photographic equipment and pockmarked suitcases. This is the kind of grandmother I want to be. A grandma nouveau.

But from a German perspective, this is quite possibly the most selfish thing a woman could do. Not only is she out spending the fruits of her life's work on silly little expeditions—rather than gathering interest on the inheritance she will leave to her children—but this grandma isn't even physically present for her family. How are they supposed to keep it together without someone guiding them, helping out?

Germans, like nationals of virtually every country outside of the United States, recognize a marriage as the tenuous link that it is. A mother's love for her children, well, that's assumed, but the *couple* needs lots of back-up support in order to grow and mature. This is where Oma comes in. She will do the laundry, the housework, the cooking, the baby-sitting, not only to help her daughter (and in Germany as in America it is still usually the daughter who is responsible for such things), but, more discreetly, to set an example of how things should be done.

This is especially true if it's the daughter-*in-law* that we're talking about. By taking over the household maintenance—particularly in all matters related to food—an Oma is saying *this is how your man should be treated. Do this, and you will keep him.* It's an unspoken bond that is passed down through the generations, woman to woman, implicitly understood and sometimes, during arguments, actually articulated. And yet, this preoccupation with keeping men happy is not born of actual love, or even respect, really, of the man himself. (The man may indeed be loved and respected, but that isn't the point.) It's simply an acknowledgment that men are necessary—they fix stuff and can carry heavy things—but, unlike women, the man's link to the world of home and hearth is not automatic. They must be constantly reminded of the good deal they're getting. Lucky for us, however, they are easily pacified with a pie or an ironed shirt.

So while the American views marriage as a lifetime love affair of epic proportions, in Germany marriage still retains an aura of pragmatism. (Which is why, when I ask Oma what is so wrong with living together instead of marrying, she doesn't talk of the flames of hell or the wrath of God, but rather points out, quite reasonably, that if a couple doesn't marry and one partner dies, the other partner won't get any money from the government.)

Because marriage is pragmatic rather than some kind of romantic adventure, it naturally follows that everyone can be a part of it. While there is something vaguely incestuous about an over-involved mother-in-law in America, the German Oma is *expected* to participate in her children's lives, however old they may be. To do otherwise would be shirking her duties, like the grandma nouveau in my daughter's storybook. In this light it makes perfect sense that my mother must call my American grandmother and get permission before she lets me stay overnight there—and my grandma may very well say no if she has other plans—but my German father never thinks to *ask* Oma if it would be all right for me to live with her for half a year purely for the experience of it. Why, that's a given.

Which, of course, gives Oma a great deal of influence. So while in America—a country that worships youth and beauty—a woman loses power as she grows older, in Germany a woman gains authority with age. She has sacrificed so much for her family that you have incurred all sorts of debts, both social and financial, that there is simply no point in giving that oh-so-American speech about it being my-life-and-I'll-do-what-I-want-with-it. Say that and she'll ask for the deed to your house, which, after all, she bought for you. (The little old women you see riding around on bicycles in Ostfriesland, cuddling their fresh bread and worrying about their potatoes burning? Most of them own a big brick house, a Mercedes, and have put six kids through college.) When her children decide to marry she will be consulted on the prospective bride or groom. Her opinion of the match will be taken very seriously, not so much out of respect for her beliefs, but because, on some level, it's her marriage, too—she'll be dropping by your house every day with fresh vegetables and if she hates your spouse, well, do you really want that kind of headache?

And so it is that the advice that they give, and give and give and give, throughout the marriage is also allowed. I scratch your back, you scratch mine. I give you this farm and babysit your kids for free instead of taking a trip around the world; you agree to live by the rules I've devised.

And whatever you do, you don't get to shoot heroin in a Berlin train station. For if you do, you'll find yourself not only dead—that's the least of your worries—but literally at her feet, the object of her wrath, her scorn, her total lack of sympathy for whatever circumstances that brought you to this pathetic point. *Drogen.* Tsk-tsk.

The cops will come eventually, I assure myself, sidestepping this fallen maiden, secretly thankful—yeah, I admit it—secretly thankful that it's not me, not only because I'm not ready to die at nineteen but because I never want to have an Oma, *anybody's* Oma, look at me that way again. Even in the afterlife. I pee quickly and run back upstairs.

"Did you find a bathroom?" Kurt asks, stomping out his cigarette and slinging his bag over his shoulder.

"Yeah," I answer. "Let's go."

The Train

By Onno Fecht
Translated by Jens Pfeifer

My father once told me a story about Tante Hilda, which she experienced during the war. Perhaps you know it already, but I'm going to tell you anyway because I think she showed a lot of courage at the time. During the war there were many prisoners of war in Germany. My father recognized them by a yellow sign on their clothes, which they called "Gelbkreuzer."

Those people had to do hard labor on the fields of Ostfriesland. My father told me that they were starving and ate the worms which came out of the soil during their digging. They were [traveling by train on the] railway tracks past Tante Hilda's parents' house. One day, one of those so-called *Gelbkreuzer* managed to escape. He jumped off the train and hid near Hilda's house in a cabbage field. Of course, they went after him. After the soldiers got him, they hit him with their rifles. Tante Hilda saw it and tried to make them stop. Today it's hard to imagine that this kind of behavior could have easily brought jail time, or worse. Anyone who raised his voice against Hitler or tried to protect a person the Nazis wanted to destroy found himself in danger.

Of course Tante Hilda couldn't rescue this prisoner, but maybe history would have been different if more people refused to silently accept injustice.

Culture Shock

By Becky Sandler

I felt honored when I was approached to share my experiences about what it was like for a Catholic to marry into a Jewish family. But the culture shock of moving from a small town to a big city makes the fact that I married into a Jewish family just the half of it!

I was born and raised in a rural community, along with two older brothers and one younger sister, on the Minnesota/North Dakota border, up near Canada. I was raised Catholic, and by that I mean *Catholic* grammar school, *Catholic* high school, attending Mass *every day* during the school year (except Saturday, when we had to go to Confession) and of course Mass every Sunday. I was pretty much ignorant of the Jewish culture and religion. Yes, there was a handful of Jews in my hometown, and even a temple. But I was unaware. I actually discovered years later that my eye doctor was Jewish, as was the owner of Silverman's, the largest men's clothing store in town.

I married a local guy in 1970 whose brother lived in the Chicago area. He always dreamed of living in a big city, so, in the spring of 1971, we moved to Chicago. Now *that* was a level of "culture shock" not easy to describe. Imagine a city of millions of people with a downtown area filled with skyscrapers, with expressways and subways and buses, being seen by a "country bumpkin" like me, who had never left the Minnesota/North Dakota area, except for a few shopping trips across the border to Winnipeg. But my husband's brother and wife helped us find a place to live, learn the city, and find a job.

After about a month, I found a job at Durkee Foods. It was very scary for me, as I was quite shy and not at all street wise, to say the least. But as time went by I started to learn the ropes, and it got a little easier. I became more comfortable and actually joined the company bowling league. That was a huge step for me, as I may have bowled once or twice before in my entire life. It was probably bumper-bowling anyway, that is if it was even invented back then!

I landed on Mike Sandler's team. It was a mixed-handicap league, and Mike was the best bowler in the company, and I was the worst, so they put us on the same team to even things out. That's actually where I got to know Mike and got my first real exposure to Judaism. The years rolled by, and every day I learned more about the city *and* the Jewish culture. I found it extremely interesting and found myself asking many questions.

Eventually, both Mike and I divorced our respective spouses, and by the late 1970s we had become "an item." I guess opposites really do attract? Country girl and city guy, Catholic and Jewish, and a rather substantial difference in age. He had a college education; I did not. He had children; I did not. But I got to know his children, Heidi and Phillip, who were approximately nine and eleven years old at the time. That, too, was a whole new experience for me. I knew that this was a package deal, and his kids were a huge part of his life, thus a huge part of mine. I look back on it now and am thankful for all the experiences I had, including their weddings and children.

We got married in 1983, after spending a week in the Bahamas. We had thought about getting married there but discovered you had to be a resident to do that. It would require a minimum of two weeks on the island, and at those prices there was no way! So we went anyway, and got married when we returned. It was kind of like taking the honeymoon before the marriage.

Next came an entire series of "firsts." I will never forget the first time I attended a Seder meal for Passover. That's when I first learned of the Jewish calendar year, that holidays run from sundown to sundown, and that Saturday was the Sabbath, not Sunday.

I will never forget when Michael stood up to take his turn reading the passages in Hebrew, as I found it quite remarkable. It rolled off his tongue as easily as English! I was amazed and highly impressed, to say the least. It is difficult enough to learn a foreign language, but learning one that uses an entirely different alphabet is beyond my comprehension. (He later confessed that he reads it phonetically, and did not understand what he was reading.) Of course, Michael being Michael, he told me ahead of time all kinds of nightmare stories about what would take place, none of which were true. I arrived at the dinner totally petrified, afraid of doing or saying something stupid. But as it turned out, his cousins Harriet and Marty and all of the family members who attended were more than gracious to me. Over time, with more and more of us "gentiles" entering the family, I actually took my turn reading the story of Passover, and Marty even let me read in English!

Then came my first Jewish funeral. That was totally strange to me. Catholic funeral services are held in a church. The wake, as it is called, is held at the funeral home, usually the evening before the funeral. The casket is usually open, and there are flowers everywhere. But this service was held at the funeral home rather than the temple, which is what I would have expected. The casket is never open, and there are no flowers.

But the most interesting part of the Jewish grieving process is called sitting *shivah*, which is the formal period of mourning that takes place in the home of the grieving family. In the Catholic religion, a funeral Mass is held, we proceed to the cemetery, have a gathering with a meal after that and that is the end of it. The family is then left alone to grieve their loved one. I think sitting *shivah* is definitely better, being surrounded by friends and family. I liked some of the other customs I was introduced to, like covering all the mirrors, as how you look is not important. I liked the symbolism of wearing the torn piece of ribbon or cloth, to signify the loss.

Then I attended my first Jewish wedding. Again I saw many differences from a Catholic wedding. What comes to mind is the canopy or *chupa* under which the bride and groom stand while taking their vows. This symbolizes the home the couple is about to create. The smashing of the glass at the end of the ceremony is also powerful—some believe that it is meant to remind everyone even in their joy about the smashing of the temple in Jerusalem. I thought it all was very fascinating, especially once you know what the rituals symbolize.

Weddings in my hometown are very different and not nearly as elaborate. Most were held on Friday evening or Saturday before sundown, which would never happen with a Jewish wedding. Besides the religious differences, there are many others. In a Catholic wedding, there's the Mass, of course, then usually a modest meal with cake and coffee immediately following the ceremony, held somewhere on the church or school property. This is referred to as the "reception." Then much later that evening, they have what is called the Wedding Dance. This is held at a hotel or banquet hall of some kind, and is much the same as what people in Chicago call the reception, and what Jewish people call the *simcha*.

The biggest difference, though, is that you don't need an invitation to attend the dance. It's open to the whole town, and as a result there's never an open bar; it's cash only. You also get a lot of people in very casual attire. Many times, the time and place of the Wedding Dance is actually published in the local newspaper so everyone knows about it. In Chicago weddings, especially Jewish ones, the reception or *simcha* is meant for family and friends only, and can be very elegant and even expensive.

Then came my first *bat mitzvah*, which is the celebration of a Jewish child becoming an adult in the eyes of the temple (*bat mitzvah* means "daughter of the commandments," while *bar mitzvah* means "son of the commandments"). The event involves a religious ceremony for which the child sometimes studies for over a year. There is often a big celebration afterwards. That was a real experience. I remember one of the first things I noticed was how elaborate the affair was. I had never even been to a wedding of that caliber.

I have learned so much more about Judaism as well, like what makes food kosher, and how is kosher for Passover different from just kosher? My first *bris* (ritual circumcision) was shocking to me. I remember thinking "that poor baby!" I learned about the different "levels" of Judaism, such as Orthodox, and Reformed. I learned that the general gentile population has difficulty determining if Judaism is a religion or a nationality. I learned that the Jewish year is a continuance of whatever the year was before the rest of the world started over in A.D. I learned of all the pain and suffering that has gone on over the decades, and have gained a great respect and understanding of Judaism as a result.

Sometimes I have difficulty determining which cultural differences I experience are because of the Jewish faith and which are simply big city versus small town, since much of the knowledge I gained and the experiences I have had over the years came from Mike and his family. All in all, the last thirty years or so have been quite a ride, and I believe that I am a different person today than I would have been had I remained in my hometown…. a different person and a better one!

The Medford Fire Department

By Ray Brost

Once a month during the summer, the Medford, WI Volunteer Fire Department would hold a Tuesday evening practice session just west of the spillway gates at the mill pond.

Things began promptly at seven p.m. The brand-new, 1946 Chevrolet fire truck was first to leave the firehouse, gliding along at a sneak, or so it seemed, because this run was done without sirens.

But then the quiet of the evening was broken anyway. A grand racket signaled that the great Pierce was on its way. This mid-1930s open-cab thoroughbred had no muffler, just a straight pipe, and its throbbing engine roared with great distinction as it swept along.

With a certain delay, as if for comic relief, the vintage Reo would then come putt-putt-putting around the corner, the several firemen in it holding their helmets on with one hand and onto the truck with the other.

In those days, fire trucks had platforms in back where firemen stood, clinging to railings. This element of show added to the merriment.

Along the narrow roadway to the gates the trucks would be lined up one behind the other, and a whir of activity followed as all sorts of tasks were carried out. You saw normally laid-back guys like Herb Bruegel, Robert Ecklund and Al Bauer running around like Keystone Kops. Hoses were dragged out and intake canisters dropped into the water. Pumps began to hum, motors revved up, and the air reverberated loudly with power and excitement. Teams of three, all in helmets, boots, and protective coats braced themselves against the push of the nozzles, whereupon you saw fountains shooting up into the blue of the evening sky, cresting in a splendid arch, then breaking into frothy white and falling like hurricane rain back into the mill pond. You wanted to see the Pierce outdo the Chevrolet as these two strove mightily to cast the highest arch of water. But the impertinent Chevrolet with its modern pump always just managed to win. In comparison, the Reo did little better than the manikin pis.

Often, right in front of us, there would be the glimpse of a rainbow! The mists created by the firemen were struck by the rays of the setting sun.

Then, too soon, the show would wind up as the fire fighters hustled around to pick up and stow away their gear. Leaving the park behind with dripping trees and soggy lawn, Medford's bravest rode triumphantly back to the firehouse where they settled down to a session of skat and sheepshead with lots of beer, crackers and Limburger cheese.

"What end do you have on the pillow?" one wife is known to have asked that same night.

Today the venerable Reo stands at rest inside the Medford Water Works Pumping Station at the edge of the city park. Whereas a handsomely-uniformed honor guard watches over Napoleon's tomb in Les Invalides in Paris, Medford's mausoleum for the Reo is secured only by a ghost—that of grim Fred Brede, unforgettable in his wide-brimmed hat and red suspenders; stubby like the cigar he was armed with, he always stood guard in the portico of the pumping station and kept a suspicious eye on any activity in the area, for example, on us kids trudging by on our way up-river for a swim.

Guns

By Habbo Fokkena

It was shortly after our arrival in Amerika that I became a gun nut. I would look at every catalog I could find, knew all the details of every gun that had ever been made, and dreamed of one day owning one myself. I started young, at the age of ten or so.

In Amerika, one begins with a BB gun. They are cheap to produce, are fairly foolproof, and are powerful enough to kill sparrows. Every boy, from the time he can read, wants a BB gun. If he is persistent enough, he can usually make his parents miserable enough that they'll give in. I was no different.

Guns are not common in Germany. In fact, very few people have them, and then only on stringent conditions. My father had owned several from his military days. I recall seeing pictures of him and of several guns he had obtained during the war. But I was born in 1947, and those guns were long gone by then. Having a gun in one's possession at the end of WWII was an offense punishable by death, and my mother wisely dumped them into the canal. Or so she says. I have seen the canal where she says she dumped them, and it is not deep enough to drown a rat. But maybe it was deeper back then.

I do remember following our local *Jaeger* (hunter) around as he went hunting. He only had one arm, and a shotgun, but he was quite good with that one arm. Perhaps that triggered my lust. Soon after we arrived in Amerika I decided that I needed to have a BB gun. My younger friend, Russ Slight, had more liberal parents, but joined in an effort to get a gun for Christmas.

First I had to listen to lectures on the dangers of shooting someone's eye out and a hundred other horror stories. But I was nothing if not persistent, and I eventually wore them down. Christmas arrived, and, there, behind the tree, was my first gun. Unfortunately it was night, and I had to wait until morning to shoot it. That was a trial.

I was up early the next morning, far earlier than ever before. It was still dark, but my parents were up and milking already. I snuck into the barn, loaded the gun, and crawled into the haymow. There, I potted a poor old pigeon too dumb to fly out. My first kill. I was ecstatic. So were the cats, who got to eat the pigeon.

Russ also got a BB gun, and in a day or two managed to come out to the farm. Alas, his parents had gotten him a better model, and I was jealous. But that passed. We then went on a reign of terror. No sparrow was safe. We counted, and, over several years, killed hundreds of them.

We did draw the line at songbirds. Sparrows, blackbirds, and the occasional pigeon were okay. But robins, red-winged blackbirds, swallows who ate mosquitoes, and finches were off-limits. We had our scruples. I remember that I once did shoot a swallow and felt guilty for weeks. I have no idea where we obtained those guidelines, but we did follow them.

I also shot targets. I had read Annie Oakley, Roy Rogers, and other cowboy stories, and those people were all crack shots. I would be, too. BBs were cheap, and on my princely allowance of twenty-five cents a week I could afford to shoot a lot. I learned to throw cans in the air, and, without aiming, hit them consistently. It helped that a BB travels relatively slowly, so in the right light one can see it fly through the air. That tracer-like effect helped train my young eyes. I can still hit cans with a BB gun or a rifle, although no doubt my skill level has, like everything else, slipped significantly.

My gun career did not end with a BB gun. I next tried for a pellet gun, then a .22 rifle, and finally, holy of holies, a shotgun. Each Christmas would lead to another pre-planned campaign of careful whining, complaining, and faithful promises to behave. Usually the campaign worked. I missed out on the pellet gun and had to suffer for a whole year, while Russell, who still came out now and then, had better success with his own whining campaign. He had a pellet gun while I did not. That grated. But I solaced myself with the knowledge that I was a better shot than he was. I still tell him that today, and, under duress, he might admit the truth of my claims.

One year I wanted a rifle, but my parents thought I was too young. My father had a habit of saving the best present until last on Christmas Eve, and I kept expecting that somewhere, somehow, a beloved gun would pop up. But it didn't happen. I cried and made everyone else's Christmas miserable. The only saving grace that year, according to my mother, was a book sent by my aunt Netti about a pet blackbird called Jacob. I eventually immersed myself in that book, laughed a lot, and my mother was eternally grateful to her sister and her fateful choice of a present. It saved Christmas that year.

Now in my old age I have many guns. I need to sell them, or give them away. My daughters are not interested in them, nor have they produced a grandson whom I can indoctrinate and thus pass on this legacy. While I still enjoy owning them—and hate to part with them—I seldom shoot anymore. I can afford to buy them now, I can shoot them now, but much of my earlier drive is spent. There is a lesson in there somewhere, but I really don't want to learn it.

Habbo Fokkena and his granddaughter, Rakaya El-Kasaby, summer 1996, on Habbo's farm four miles north of Clarksville, Iowa.

When I was twenty-four, I spent a weekend on my dad's farm watching him plant trees. This was pretty mundane, seeing as how he'd been doing it since I was a kid and it was boring to do and even more boring to watch. Guy digs hole, guy inserts sapling, guy covers hole, lather, rinse, repeat. "I'm building a windbreak," he used to say when I was little. I didn't care about wind, much less the act of breaking it. We lived on a hill, and, when I was a kid, our house was surrounded by this line of tiny evergreens that were neither pretty nor functional. The only good trees on our land were the ones in the meadow, the ones my grandfather had planted. By the time I was ten they were big enough for climbing, ergo they were, by definition, good trees.

But watching him I realized that both my dad and grandfather had taken the long view. They were expending this impossible amount of sweat on something that wouldn't pay off in their lifetimes, much less by the end of the semester, but they did it anyway because it needed doing. I climbed the trees my grandfather planted even as he was too sick to take a walk without getting lost, or feed himself with a spoon. And now I was sitting on the porch of this old farmhouse surrounded by full-grown evergreens, trees that grew right up year after year whether I was in high school or college or Egypt. That old house now has a windbreak.

~Laura Fokkena

The Doghouse

By Habbo Fokkena

We always had dogs while living on the farm. In Germany dogs were a luxury and had to be tied up all the time. But on a farm, a dog is a dog, not a pet. After we finally got on our own land in 1956, our sponsor told us we needed a dog. He brought over Jim, a big German shepherd police dog. We were told that he would protect us, and though we weren't sure what we needed to be protected from, we obligingly took him home.

Any dog is a ten-year-old's dream. You can talk to your dog and tell him things no one else needs to know. The dog will always be there, always ready to go for a walk, always cheerful. I had never had a dog before, so Jim was something new.

I tried to teach Jim tricks. But the only thing he knew how to do was shake hands, and he already knew that when he came. Dogs should be able to herd cows, I thought, and help me get them back from the pasture. But Jim was not a herding dog, and the cows did not like him. Whenever he was around they were nervous. Perhaps he looked too much like a wolf and their primal instincts told them something was amiss when there was this type of animal around.

But Jim did like to dig holes and chase animals. He and I explored our new kingdom. We investigated all the ditches and junk piles. I remember he caught a possum once. It was my first contact with a wild animal and I was amazed.

Jim did not stay around for long. We lived on a busy road and one day a car hit him. I don't recall the details anymore, but he was gone. But then we had the opportunity to acquire our very own, beginning-from-scratch dog. Flockie arrived.

Our Flockie was not the first Flockie. Our father had regaled us all our lives with the tricks and wonders of his first dog. Apparently, when he was young, he had gotten a small terrier. It had to be small, since I very much doubt his household back then would have allowed a large dog that ate too much. But his Flockie was Flockie the Wonder Dog. He would retrieve sticks, speak, and do all sorts of wonderful things. Now, in adulthood, I sense this dog was a welcome companion to my father, who had lost his mother, had many siblings, a new stepmother, and a tiny house. Flockie was probably his one luxury and faithful companion. It's no wonder Flockie assumed mythical proportions.

So when the time came to receive our very own young puppy, who had no name, she became Flockie also. Flockie was a mix of many dogs, a real Heinz 57 variety. She had some sheepdog, and some border collie, but was shorter and fatter than a Lassie dog. But she was all ours.

Flockie was not the brightest dog around, and never did learn any of the tricks of her namesake. She would not fetch, no matter how hard we tried to teach her. She was not good at herding cows, either, although the cows were not as nervous around her as they had been with Jim. Neither was she a hunter. She did not point, hold, nor retrieve. If I shot a rabbit she would just eat it or run away with it. I think the only trick she ever learned was how to shake hands, and to sit.

But Flockie loved us, especially Willie and me. Initially I did more with her (or tried to, anyway), but as I grew into adolescence and found other interests she became a closer companion to Willie. He, like I, no doubt grew to appreciate her friendliness and her willingness to go anywhere, any time.

Flockie also became important when my maternal grandparents came to visit for their first and only time in Amerika. In Germany, grandparents are Opas and Omas. Since we had four, we distinguished them not by their first or last names, but by where they lived. So my mother's parents became Oma and Opa Walle, and the other set were Oma and Opa Georgsheil. I have no idea where this custom started, but they were the only names by which I knew them as a small child, and they are still referred to in that fashion some thirty years after their deaths.

Our Opas and Omas did not travel, unlike their children, grandchildren, and great-grandchildren, so when they came to visit it was a big deal. Flockie played her part. She was finally to receive something I felt she should have: a real doghouse!

You must understand dogs do not, in proper German farmhouses, live inside. Dogs are dogs, and their place is outside. The only exception might be in the winter, when they could sleep in the barn or in the hog house. But never in the house. Their place was under the porch, on the porch, or on the inevitable rug just outside the door.

And buying a doghouse is out of the question. Why waste perfectly good money on a dog? That would be a sin of major proportions. But building a doghouse out of scrap lumber is okay; that only is good sense, since something practical is built out of something that would otherwise go to waste. So I had tried to build a doghouse for her.

But my dad was not a carpenter. He had not learned practical things like working with wood, or, more importantly, working with cars and mechanical things. He could cook, he could do amazing math in his head, he would work hard all day, but he was not a carpenter. So I did not pick up any such skills, and still don't possess them today. It's a life lesson. If your mother or father don't possess certain skills that they think should be known to every boy or girl, then you won't have them either, unless you must acquire them later in life when you have no choice. But Opa Walle was a carpenter by trade. We all knew that. Finally, Flockie was going to receive her just desserts, a real castle of a doghouse.

Poor Opa Walle had no idea he was expected to perform this miraculous feat. He arrived, befuddled and tired from the long trip, and must have been surprised to hear our plans for how he was to spend his vacation. We could not wait for him to start. Expectations were high.

Opa tried. We did have scrap lumber, some saws, and a few leftover nails. But I think our materials were not of the quality he was used to, and I expect he was not as excited as we were about his task. But, spurred on by our urgings, he performed his Opaly task, and built us a doghouse.

It was Flockie-sized, with a rounded front door and a pitched roof just like a real house. Finally, she would have her castle! We could not wait to have her inspect her quarters.

But then came the great disappointment. Flockie had no interest in her house! It was summer, and she much preferred the outside rug or, if it was raining, the shed. We tried everything. We pushed her into it. We tied her up in it and left her there. The poor dog probably figured she had done something wrong. But she refused to go into the doghouse on her own free will.

I'm not sure exactly what else we did when Opa and Oma Walle visited us. I'm sure we visited people, had company, had many long talks, and various other things. I can still see them there, though I can't recall much else from their visit. But I do remember Flockie's doghouse.

Flockie stayed with us a long time. She did not get run over, even though I think she was nicked once by a car. She never did anything exceptional. But she was ours, and she loved us.

Flockie moved with the family to the new farm in 1964. I left to attend college, but Willie was still young. He remained her closest friend. When Flockie finally died and did not show up, Willie searched for her for days. She was mourned by him more than anyone else.

Since Flockie left, I, too, have regaled my children with Flockie tales. I have tried to get them to name our parade of dogs with her distinguished moniker.

But they will have none of that. In Amerika, a dog named Flockie does not fit in. It is too easy to drop the "l" in her name, and then people might think strange thoughts when you call for your dog. So we had dogs named Nick, Ivy, Blackie, Simba, and Nala. But no more Flockies. She has passed on into the mists of dogdom history. But she is not forgotten.

Oma Walle

By Clara (Fokkena) Hinman

June 28, 2004

Dear Laura, Lisa, and Rakaya,

A year ago at this time we went to Germany. It had been thirty-five years since I first went to Ostfriesland. Of course, I didn't know you then, but I knew Habbo's Oma Walle, so I will tell you about her.

Oma Walle was really Gertje Lüken, but I knew her as Oma Walle because she was the grandmother who lived in the village of Walle.

When Habbo and I first arrived by train in Leer, Onkel Arnulf picked us up and took us to Oma Walle's house. She and Tante Netti were standing at the end of the barn. Oma was dressed in black because her husband had died two years before. She was very stooped and she wore her long hair in a little bun. She greeted us cheerfully, and we went into the house for tea and strawberry torte.

During the years of 1968 and 1969 we made six trips to Ostfriesland. We went back again in the summer of 1971. Each time we left, Oma was sure we would never see her again. It was sad to leave her, but happily she was there each time we returned.

Oma's house and barn were connected. When I was shown the barn, I was told about the outhouse at the end of it. I thought it was convenient to be able to go from the house to the outhouse without going outside. I had gone to an outhouse through all kinds of Iowa weather until I was fourteen.

There were large stacks of peat in the barn. It was used for fuel in Oma's cook-stove all year. The stove also provided hot water in a little reservoir at one side, and it provided heat in the winter. Oma Walle's special chair was at an angle at the side and front of the stove. The peat for the stove was close at hand. When I was growing up in Iowa, one of my chores was to carry oil from barrels behind the house to the barrel that attached directly to the stove. The whole process had to be done outside. Once again I thought Oma Walle's attached barn was very convenient. Last summer I was happy to see Horst had restored the stove.

The first room inside the back door of Oma Walle's house was a kitchen used only in the summer. I remember being told not to throw dish water or anything else down the cistern outside the back door, where rainwater collected to be used later.

Even though Oma Walle and I didn't speak the same language, we communicated. Often we had the help of Dagmar or Habbo. Other times it didn't seem to matter if we were alone without an interpreter. I remember times we were alone and the two of us would sit in her living room having tea. She had memorized very long poems which she would recite. It didn't matter that I didn't understand. There was such feeling in her voice and it was something special to be there. Sometimes she would continue talking while it became dark, and she saw no reason for light. There would be a shocking change in mood when someone would come in and suddenly turn on the light.

When we went back to Walle at Christmas, the room that had been Opa Walle's carpentry shop had been turned into a bathroom. It was very nice, but I don't think anyone ever understood how convenient I thought that toilet in the barn was.

All of us, including Oma Walle, went to the Georg Kittel store before Christmas. Oma wanted us to pick out a pattern for silverware. Oma was led to a room away from the front of the store where she could sit down and look at patterns. We picked the pattern that was unique to the area.

Oma had a Christmas tree on a table in the living room near the window. She told me red candles looked best on the tree in the daytime, and white candles looked best at night. They were lit while we sang in the evening.

In the evening Oma, Tante Hanni, Tante Netti, Dagmar, Habbo, and I were at Oma's house. Onkel Arnulf was with his mother in Heidelberg because his father had died the previous year. Later Garrelt came with his two-and-a-half-year-old twins, Onno and Gesa. We sang the same songs I remembered from the previous Christmas with Habbo's parents at the farm south of Clarksville. "Kling, Glöckchen, Kling" will always remind me of sixteen-year-old Dagmar.

"O Du Fröhliche" reminds me of Habbo's father. I can hear his deep voice singing it yet. Last summer Garrelt played "O Du Fröhliche" for me in his front yard on the harmonica. At first he said he wouldn't because it wasn't Christmas, but I reminded him that I wouldn't be there at Christmas.

There was a pasture that came within a few feet of Oma's living room window. Oma had one cow in the pasture in the summers. She milked it twice a day. When it was time for milking, the cow stood directly in line with Oma's window and appeared to look inside. There were people who stopped by Oma's house to buy the milk. She kept a bowl of cream on the table for tea and covered it with a cloth.

There was a time Oma showed us what she wanted to wear to be buried in. I remember it as a kind of shroud. She also showed us where she would be buried, and she took comfort in knowing she would be between her husband and her mother. Last summer I had a chance to put flowers there.

I remember Oma showing us her *gute Stube*, her good living room which could be reached only by going through either of two bedrooms. It was so unused that it seemed like a secret room. Now Horst and Gesa live in the house and have remodeled it. Walls have been removed and the tea table is near where the *gute*

Stube had been. As Gesa served tea to us and her little Ilva, I felt Oma Walle's presence and I felt she was satisfied.

Gesa Fecht serves cake to her daughter, Ilva Lückemeyer, and her niece Rakaya El-Kasaby.

My cousin Gesa inherited Habbe and Gertje Lüken's house in Walle. She and her husband, Horst—a carpenter—are restoring it. I remember visiting Oma Walle's house when I was four years old; it is one of my earliest and most joyful memories. The featherbed was my favorite place to play or hide. In spring of 2004, thirty-two years later, I watched my own children (Katie and Joey and their friend Emily Loar) play in that house, on different furniture, within newly-built walls, but with the same joy.

~Heidi Sandler

Birds

By Jens Pfeifer

Whenever I'm back home after a visit at my grandmother's these days, I'm filled with nostalgic and sentimental emotions. I'm writing this because some of you might be interested in this and in fact I should have written it years ago. And I'm writing it in English not because it's easier for me, but because I don't feel very familiar with my mother language either. So, mistakes are sort of allowed this way.

In front of me, just next to the computer monitor, lies a handmade pouch that she did as a young girl (maybe when she was eighteen). That would be almost seventy years ago. It's made of jute and the side of the clasp looks like the surface of a quilt.

You won't believe what's in there! But I'll tell you. There is a one billion mark bill. There are parts of a newspaper dated Sunday, 22 April, 1945. There's a newspaper dated 14 September, 1961, with the obituaries for my grandfather. There's my grandfather's salary statement from May, 1957. There's a letter to my grandmother written by her grandmother when she was about eighty. And I could go on like that.

When I stepped into her living room tonight she was about to sort out old documents, photos, and newspapers, just like she wanted to say "I don't have much time left" but then I reassure myself that she's been telling us this for the past fifteen years now. And while she takes out every single thing that's in that pouch, she starts to tell stories. Some of them I hear for the third or fourth time, but that's okay, because my Oma is an excellent storyteller.

My Oma had a younger brother called Bernhard. He was born when she was three years old, always weak and shy and dependent on his mother. At the age of five he claimed that he had to get up when the snowdrops open their blossoms and that he had to go to bed when they had closed them again.

At the age of six he died.

Two days before he was sitting in front of his window and he noticed a little bird which was flying around just outside that window. This must have been one

141

of the early birds because it was only February. So he asked Gerta (my Oma) to catch that bird and bring it inside. My Oma did like she was told and she was surprised when the bird didn't even get ready to escape. Without any effort she could take it and put it into a little box. This box had to be placed right next to Bernhard's bed.

The bird sang for him.

The next day Bernhard decided that the bird wanted to get out of the cage. All present family members went outside to see Gerta open the cage. Then something strange happened. The bird sat down at the edge of the cage and then flew straight up to the sky. Bernhard just said: "Look, Mommy, that's the way I will go to heaven."

The next day when my Oma came home from school, Bernhard had died.

Lisa Fokkena with Gerta Pfeifer and her godmother, Netti Henke. Aurich, summer 2003.

In Boston we have our groceries delivered. Most of it is processed food or meat that has been around since the birth of Christ. While we were staying in Aurich, however, the refrigerator was too small to hold a serious supply of food, so every morning I would get up, survey its contents, decide what the Fokkena women I was living with would actually eat, and then go into town—walking past the castle (!), past the medieval statue (!), to the bakery for fresh (!) bread, and then to the butcher shop for fresh (!) meat. One morning I arrived to find the whole street filled with vendors. It was a farmer's market, which they apparently have twice a week in Aurich. I bought some fish from the North Sea, so fresh its mother would have recognized it. The Fokkena women eschewed it in favor of wine and German chocolate, but I didn't mind. I decided I wanted to live in a country where people took their grocery shopping seriously.

~Connor Durflinger

Dagmar and Maike Albers on the coast of the North Sea, June, 1986. The sea is a powerful symbol in the songs and folklore of the region.

Ostfriesland is a beautiful part of Germany. The people, the land with its wind-bent trees, the dikes, and the many islands with their screeching seagulls are what gets into your blood. You simply cannot forget a freshly-plowed field in preparation for planting potatoes, the green meadows filled with wildflowers such as "Korblumen," and the sometimes angry clouds that appear when a storm approaches. The climate can be rough, influenced by the Nordsee with its everchanging "Ebbe" and "Flut." Some of us draw strength from the sea, and it is said that women's cycles are affected by the rhythm of the waves. A song in Plattdeutsch comes to mind: "Wor de Nordseewellen trecken an de Strand, wor de geelen Blöme bleuhn int gröne Land, wor de Möven schrieen gell in Stromgebrus, dor is meene Heimot, dor bun ick to huus."

~Gerda Taylor

A Life

By Dagmar Albers
Translated by Gerda Taylor

On the 80th birthday of her father, Arnulf Henke:

Dear Papa,

A birthday is without question the nicest day to honor someone by celebrating and reflecting back on all the years. An 80th birthday is definitely a milestone and a special day to say "Thank You" for so many things.

Dear Papa, as I reflect on all the wonderful things you have done for me and for the family, I will try to list some special dates and remember accomplishments in your life.

You were always "Papa," "Paps," "Papi," or "Nuff-Puff" to me, a man who was not only a father but also a companion and leader as I tried to find my way in the world. I thank God that you are still that person for me today.

The world we live in is a difficult one and without someone to show us the way it becomes a struggle to stay on the right path. You were there from the start to pave the way in a guiding, loving way.

It was difficult for you to let go of the "child" that needed to cut the apron strings and go out into the world. You and Mom raised me in a way that enabled me to become strong enough to master the difficulties that came my way.

You were born on a Sunday in the early afternoon as the second child to your parents in the town of Kiejsze in Poland. When you were two years old, you and your parents moved to Izbica (we still have a picture of you wearing a "dress").

You grew up in a Christian home and at the age of six your father enrolled you in his school (a Protestant school) where he taught you religion. Your teachings were in the Polish language, a language you still master.

You transferred to a Polish Gymnasium in 1935 in Leslau and needed to live in a "Waisenhaus" (a home for orphans) since this was far from your parents' home. You wore a school uniform. You transferred again in 1939 to Lyceum where you graduated from a school, which prepared you for your Abitur. This became difficult because the Second World War began and you needed to wait until 1941 to finish your education. Your dream had always been to study and become a veterinarian. This had to be put on the backburner and you worked in a government office to earn your first paycheck! In 1941 you were ordered to the military and began building train tracks. In 1942 you were ordered to work for the air force in Poland. In 1944 you enrolled in a school to become a pilot and after twenty test flights you succeeded in your mission. Through many trials and tribulations and many stations in Germany you arrived in Gardelegen, Holland where you became employed as an accountant.

In 1945 (when the war was over) your journey took you to Ostfriesland for the first time and to the town of Westermarschpolder. From there it was not far to Walle where a beautiful woman took your breath away and from that point on you did not want to leave Ostfriesland anymore! In October of that year you were released from the military (Bundeswehr) and tried once again to study to become a veterinarian. It did not happen; instead your education continued in teaching and in 1948 you passed all your tests in Hannover and became a teacher.

You married in 1948 and taught school in a town near Varel, Germany, while living in a tiny place (without a bathroom) way under the rafters of this very school.

I, Dagmar, was born in 1952.

It seemed that school and studies were not over for you. Your interest was in teaching handicapped children and of course you succeeded and passed all the needed tests. You bought a home. Finally a house of our own! You built a garage with your own hands and laid out a beautiful vegetable garden. A car was bought and the first trip you and your little family made was of course to Ostfriesland!

Later you were offered a position as a special teacher for handicapped children (Sonderlehrer) in Aurich! My grandparents offered you a piece of land, on which you built a beautiful home and once again you built a beautiful garden. Later you moved your family again and now live in Aurich, Graf-Ulrich-Strasse 17.

I, Dagmar, met a young man who was also born in Ostfriesland and we married and gave you a granddaughter. Her name is Maike. When your son-in-law died at a very early age in 1984 you once again assumed responsibility as a grandfather and asked us to move in with you and Mom. You were there when Maike became ill, needed fatherly advice, or just a pair of extra arms to offer love.

Dad, you simply had no time to grow "old"…..

Doing the Dishes

By Phil Sandler

A trembling in his hand as he lifts the fat wooden pipe to his lips. I can see how old and wrinkled that hand has become. How many years have the wrinkles been there? I can't remember. It seems that his hands, his face, his entire body have not changed for as long as I've known him. He always looked the same to me, from the time he was teaching me how to catch with my first baseball mitt until my mother's funeral. He is still the same figure of a man. The same person in my life.

But here's a new picture for the family album. Here's my father, lighting the dope pipe. At the age of twenty-one a man has the right to get drunk with his father. I guess at forty-three he has the right to get his father high. Not that it's his first time; he's done it before, maybe not a lot, but a few times at least. He was around during the seventies, and he knows what's what. Not to say that this isn't as unique an experience to him as it is to me. I was his first, and only, child.

He starts to take his first hit off the pipe, and it's real obvious that he doesn't do this very often. He doesn't put the end in his mouth, just presses it up against his lips, like he's afraid of getting my germs or something. He also forgets to have the lighter ready in his other hand, so he's got to start all over again. A fascinating thing, watching your father light a dope pipe. Almost like a dream; here's this guy that's raised you since you were a baby, and he's flicking a powder blue lighter and putting the flame to an illegal green substance. Inhaling. This is my father! My father is smoking marijuana with his little boy. He's also smoking the marijuana his little boy bought, and paid a lot of money for. Well, let it never be said that I don't provide my family with the very best things in life.

And it is good stuff, maybe the best I ever had. Even as he passes me the pipe, with his cheeks puffed and his face burning red from holding in the smoke, I can see the effect it is starting to have on him. The stuff is such a great high, it makes you feel like you're glowing. Not that I do it all that much; it's more of a weekend thing for me. As for my father, well, we had a little conversation about a week ago. A sort of confession. We talked about all the little things we've done in our lives, things that aren't exactly bad, but aren't great either. Like cheating, fighting, shoplifting. Guy stuff. Anyway, each of us admitted to having smoked before (I didn't tell him I do it regularly), so we decided we'd do it together, just once. You know, just for the hell of it. For fun.

So now I've got the pipe and the lighter and my dad can't hold it in a second longer; he's gagging and coughing and the smoke is spurting uncontrollably from his mouth and nose. His face is bright red and contorted and the veins in his neck are standing out obscenely. He looks like a sick, ancient dragon. Christ, I think, maybe this isn't such a grand idea, he's not a kid anymore. But he regains control of his breathing and smiles at me. His stringy white hair is sticking straight up over his bald spot, and half his collar is on the inside of his shirt. Man, does he look funny! Like one of those hopeless fellows you see on the street, who seem to have forgotten where they live. I haven't even taken a hit yet and I hardly even recognize the old guy.

But I'm not about to let such good stuff burn on its own. I take a big, big toke and watch as the green unfurls in a blaze of orange. The smoke pours into my lungs with all its burning sweetness—this is really good stuff, so smooth that you don't know you're getting any until your lungs are full. And then that feeling of light-headedness, that feeling that is your body telling you to exhale before you die. But I hold it in, keeping my eyes on the bowl instead of passing it back, knowing that if I look at my father I'll lose it. It's a nice old wooden bowl, with a flat top and a rounded bottom. The sides are carved in some sort of intricate pattern—I never really bothered to look at the carvings, but they are there. I've always thought of the pipe (I've had it a long, long time) as more of a utilitarian item than a thing of beauty. Still, it is quite nicely made. Rather more like an ornate piece you would find in an antique store than a device used for smoking grass.

Dad wants another hit. Can't blame him. Even with good weed it takes two or three hits to really get going, but this is top-of-the-line stuff. One hit is all it takes, and from the amount he was coughing, I could tell that his first hit was a good one. But I humor him, pass him back the pipe and the whole scene repeats itself: the goofy way he handles the pipe, his forgetfulness with the lighter, the heart-wrenching way he coughs, gags. Then he passes the pipe back to me. Don't do it, I say to myself. But what the hell, I take another hit, knowing how far away it's going to send me.

I've got to get up, get some water. I know it has to be now because in five minutes I won't be able to stand. I go into the kitchen, careful not to trip over anything, I trip a lot in this condition. My father's dish cabinet: empty. My father never, ever does the dishes. The only time they ever get done is when I come over and do them. I've done them a handful of times in the two years he's had the place. I tell him and tell him, but he insists that it's his place, that he pays the rent and if he doesn't want to do the dishes, they'll just have to stay dirty. It's not one of my favorite arguments. I turn on the water, pick up the dingy-brown soap pad. Soap? The last time I was over it was almost gone. Where does he keep the extra dish soap? Back in the living room: "Dad, where do you keep the dish soap?"

He looks up and smiles at me. "Oops," he says. I have never seen such a grin on his face before. Such a contented, happy, goofy-ass grin. Not even when my mother was alive. He looks like he just got every present on his Christmas list, and a few extra ones he hadn't dared ask for. Yep, forget it, he's out there. Gone. He's simply glowing, like he just got superlaid by a supermodel. I can feel my own blood start pulsing. Bump-bump, bump-bump. I have to sit down; my legs are starting to feel weak. Bump-bump, bump-bump. Forcing me to close my eyes, sit back, and just feel.

A few minutes later. The initial tidal wave of pleasure has passed, but there's still plenty of good feeling. I'm still sitting with my eyes closed, leaning back into the couch. I've almost forgotten my father is even here, until he speaks. "Christ, I'm thirsty." I get up again, forgetting that not only are there no clean glasses, but there is also nothing to clean them with. I check the refrigerator for pop, juice, anything. Empty. How does this man live?

"Dad," I yell from the kitchen, "where the hell's the extra dish soap?"

It takes him a moment to answer. "Let's go to the store," is his unsubtle answer. He doesn't have any. We're going to have to drive to the store, in our condition, just to get some soap to wash a glass to drink this dry, pasty sensation off our lips? Just because my father didn't think far enough ahead to buy a bottle of dish soap when his old bottle was starting to get low? Maybe he should just move in with my family; he obviously can't get things straight anymore. Not even sober! Now one of us has to get behind the wheel of a car with an illegal drug running through our blood. Yep, let's go for a ride. A ride in the family car.

As soon as the front door opens and my father feels the cool night air on his face, he takes off running. My seventy-one year old father. I can't chase after him, not in my condition, so I figure I'll just meet him at the car. I hope he doesn't forget about me and drive to the store by himself. Lord have mercy on the store people if he does. The air feels great, running all over my body like the hands of a lover. A good lover. A wild erotic lover. I can barely stand, it feels so good. I stop and sway, just standing under the open sky in the beautiful night air without a worry in the world, alone with myself, with my good feeling and my blood pounding. I just stand there, enjoying the everything and the nothing. But only for a moment, because a set of lights go on in the parking lot and I have to sprint to the side of the car.

I look in the driver's side window and there he is. His head is resting on the top of the steering wheel, and his right hand is trying to jam the keys in the ignition. I try to open the door, but he's locked it ("A good habit to get into," he used to tell me). I knock on the window, and he rolls it down angrily. Our faces are about six inches apart and again I am struck by how wrinkled he has become. In the reflecting light of the headlights, with our faces so close, he looks so worn. His eyes are red-rimmed, and I can hear the rasp of his breathing. When did my father get old? I don't remember it happening. But he's seventy-one. Seventy-one! The dope helps me realize it, accept it. My father is old.

"Dad…" I start to say, remembering why I knocked on the window.

"Jesus H. Christ! My damn car keys won't go in! American engineering, hah!" He's still trying to jam the keys in. Pretty soon one of them will break.

I'm afraid if I smile gently at him, it will hurt his feelings. How long has he been like this? Is it the dope making him this way, or is the dope just making me see it for the first time? It's sad either way. I do us both a favor and yell at him: "Dad, for God's sake, that's not your car! Now get out of there before someone comes!" He scrambles around and out of the car, beeping the horn briefly. He hands me the keys and climbs into his own car, on the passenger side. Guess I'm driving. I get in and he's sitting there staring out the window. He won't look at me, and my guess is he's pissed. Then I hear a little snort and a chuckle and the next thing I know he's giggling like a little boy, holding his sides and slapping his knee. It really is pretty funny, and the weed helps me laugh a little too.

Inside the store, he's a holy terror. It's not just the smoke, he's like this all the time; I've been shopping with him before. He makes a beeline for the soap aisle—he knows where everything is, he's an expert shopper, which makes a man wonder why there's no food in his refrigerator. My father will not, *will not* buy anything not on sale. It's his life now, clipping coupons and watching the newspapers for big sales. "2 for $2" the sign says. My father picks up one bottle and heads straight for the checkout. As he passes me he whispers "two for two bucks," as if he's found King Tut's tomb! As if the sign isn't right there, in plain sight for the world to see! I know there is an embarrassing scene coming and I am helpless to stop it, because on top of everything else I'm starting to get the giggles. Big time.

My dad walks right up to the counter as if he owns the place. I scoot through to the other side of the checkout, so that I can run, if necessary. He sets the bottle down on the conveyor belt with a thud, and all I can do is think "thank God it's late and nobody's here, thank God it's late and nobody's here." The lady at the register says good evening, to which my dad answers, rather smartly too, that he is buying dish soap, *this* bottle of dish soap, and he wants the sale price. I am biting the insides of my cheek to keep from laughing. Unsuccessfully. My body is shaking, tears are streaming down my cheeks. Now he tells her not to try and "gyp" him, because he knows someone from the FDA (he means the Better Business Bureau, and he is also lying). This scene could go on for hours if I don't intervene, but I can't, because I know that if I open my mouth, obnoxious laughter will emerge.

The lady pulls the bottle across the electronic eye, and the computer intones: "One-dol-lar-and-fif-ty-nine-cents." I knew it was going to happen. I do all my shopping at this store (my house and my father's apartment are only a few miles distant). When a sale price says "2 for" or "3 for" or whatever, you don't get the reduced price when you buy just one. My father's face just opens. There is nothing in his face that resembles rational thought. He stands in shock. The lady tells him his total, but he just stands there, doing nothing. Finally he says, "Your goddamn computer just gypped me out of that sale! Jesus Christ! Before they had these computers, a guy could get a sale if a store was having one. God dammit, I wanna talk to your manager!" And on and on.

I am far removed from the whole scene. I feel like I am standing back, watching a really good comedian do an imitation of what my father will be like in thirty years. It's funny, too. The laughter I was holding in spills over and becomes audible. I laugh and snort, egged on by the dope and what goes on before me. The store manager comes over to the checkout, and now the insanity reaches a new level. My father tells the manager that crooked businesses always go under. The manager is trying to be reasonable, trying to cool my father off. My father will have none of it. He stands right in the store manager's face and hollers that he knows all about the bait and switch, and he's not going to fall for it. I am clutching my sides, stomping my feet. No one notices, I'm too far away. It's so unreal seeing this: my father, making a fool out of both of us in a local supermarket. Raising a stink. Giving them hell. My old man. My old man.

Then it all unwinds before me. I see it as it really is. My father, my father, arguing over sixty cents as if his life depends on it. He's standing there yelling at the store manager, yelling at the top of his lungs. I can't believe it. Unreal. The store manager is trying to explain the store policy to him, but he just doesn't get it. I can see it in his face. He just plain doesn't understand. The register lady is rolling her eyes. Listen to this crazy old coot, her expression says, boy, someone should call the funny farm. I don't feel like laughing anymore. I feel more like crying, like burying my face in my hands and running out. Running home sobbing, to find the one person who always understood my problems, who was always there when I needed him, who could always make it better. But I know I can't. He's gone.

"It's all right, Dad," I say, stepping forward. The lady gives me a look that says *what the hell took you so long.* I narrow my eyes at her. I hand over the money and get my change, keeping my arm around my father's shoulders. I smile at him reassuringly.

"You know," the store manager whispers, as if my father isn't even there, "he really shouldn't be out by himself."

"Shut up," I say nastily, and immediately feel bad. "Let's go, Dad." My arm still around him as I lead him out. Back in his apartment, I will do the dishes.

Never Gonna Die

By Willie Fokkena

Stoned out, floating high
Got to be great
Never gonna die
Colorful patterns, crimson and clean
Beautiful people, no more tears
A buzzen sound in my ears
I ain't got no more fears
Stoned out, floating so high
I can fly
All over the shifting sky
And I'm never gonna die.

Arnulf Henke, his sister Hildegard, and Netti Henke in an outdoor café on the North Sea island of Langeoog. Summer, 2003.

It was easy to recall one of the longest times I had ever spent with Uncle Arnulf—the time we played chess. Tante Netti and my grandma Clara were conversing, German and English. Uncle Arnulf set up the chess board and we played while sipping some ginger ale. We kept each other going for about an hour. After every turn I wondered if he was letting me win or really playing, as somehow I had not yet lost, but not yet won. I wasn't very good at chess. Finally we ended at a draw, but with our kings left. He moved his king towards mine and said I had won.

~Rakaya El-Kasaby

For My Mother On Her 80th Birthday

By Dagmar Albers
Translated by Jens Pfeifer

Priorities

Almost everyone has something in life that brings particular enjoyment. For you it has been your family.

Values are not there by themselves, they are not inborn or a matter of course, but rather have to be created and renewed constantly. "Your property is what you don't carry within yourself," said Matthias Claudius.

Art objects, antiques, and jewelry weren't important to you. Important was harmony in your family. You put everything you had into that.

There were many material comforts. I remember the mechanical mixer that you once won. But those things were never important to you.

Never in your life did you change your perfume. As long as I can remember, my mother will always have the flavor of lavender. You could proudly show off your skin: so very few creases, which can only be the result of the constant use of "Oil of Olaz." We should think about advertising.

Was there anything special you'd like to have, but did not get?

Holidays

How much space should a chronicle save for this chapter?

One person wants to take extended vacations in one place; another is fond of constant roaming. You loved to travel to many different places, places that would take your breath away. London, Paris, Moscow remind us of eventful days. It was exciting to experience different cultures.

But you also took us to Linsengericht, Borkum, the Lago Maggior, the Canary Islands and the Balearic Islands, enriched many church trips and made the holidays convenient for us. We even went to the United States a couple of times, on

For My Mother On Her 80th Birthday

the trails of our grandparents, or to visit relatives. Whether we went hiking in the mountains or on holiday at the seaside, whenever we got back home your first words were always: *Thank God, we are back home safe and healthy.*

Sports

You were not an active athlete who took part in competitions. But you passionately took part in your grandchild's horseback riding. Her bruises were cooled by your hand.

Celebrations

Not everyone likes to celebrate special events with passion. *I'm turning eighty, so what? Fifty-year anniversary; praise the Lord I'm allowed to experience it.* Unforgettable memories will accompany you along your way. Christenings, weddings, and other great days. A life without celebrations is like a life without a *Gasthaus*, Democritus said 460 years before Christ. You lived by the following saying:

> *always joyful is dangerous*
> *always sad is arduous*
> *always happy is deceitful*
> *every now and then is pleasant*

We wish you many more celebrations and good health among your beloved ones.

Health

"Mix action and inaction, then you'll stay healthy."

A chapter that gives one reason to be happy and thankful, but also makes one sigh.

For you it meant a life of withstanding the pain that so frequently appeared. Surely you won't forget those days of adversity, but a gracious, forgiving memory—and despite everything, the luck of stable health—make it possible for you to be so active in your old age, the way you are today. We all thank God for that and ask him to do the best He can to preserve your iron will even on bad days. But allow yourself a break every once in a while, because you've missed it for so many years.

Surprises

Where there any surprises in your life, positive or negative?

"Behind every corner there are many different directions."

Sure, but which ones?

Well, you must know best the point your path took an unexpected turn. Your daughter came back to your house after many years. Your son-in-law passed away too early and taking in a three-year-old child was an unexpected but tempting and, at the end of the day, worthwhile task…Wasn't it?

We hope that you, the center of our family, the one who didn't take the path to retirement but rather the hectic, innovative, and restless way of a companion to a young family, can say today: How could I have grown old except in this way, being needed all the time, even though I sometimes didn't want to spend my life running around and checking the roads for potholes and danger signs, even though I might have preferred to just ride along and enjoy the view?

"Get used to nothing and everything stays exceptional," said K.H. Waggerl, 1950.

You could surely sign your name to that.

Meetings

"You recognize a secure friend when you're in an insecure situation," said Cicero, many years before Christ.

You met with many people in your long life who made a special impression on you. You got to know them quickly but intensively, and they told you the story of their lives.

Some quick meetings can later become valuable relationships. Some friends had to pass away already and are not with us anymore. Take your time to think about them and the good times you spent together.

Hobbies

Some hobbies like gardening, swimming, and reading remained true to you over the years. You became a specialist in riddles. Time for hobbies and activities remained a foreign concept to you for many years. Take your time for them now.

I would like to close this small and surely not comprehensive chronicle of your life with the Biblical saying:

> *Unser Leben wahret 70 Jahre*
> *und wenn es hoch kommt,*
> *so sind es 80 Jahre,*
> *und wenn es köstlich gewesen ist,*
> *so sind es Mühe und Arbeit gewesen.*

The writer thanks for your patience and hopes to learn even more about you in future conversations. She hopes to have you here on earth at her side for many more years.

God's blessings for the coming years, and health and peace of mind to give your descendants even more of your wisdom and cleverness.

Yours,
Dagmar

The Flowers In My Mother's Yard

By Willie Fokkena

The flowers in my mother's yard
All crimson, green, and gold.
They seem to speak of something
That one in his hand can't hold.

When evening brings the misting dawn
And everywhere I see
The gentle caressing colors of
The garden serenity.

Then is when life seems to be
Worth the toil of the day.
When one can walk through his mother's yard
And ease the pain away.

Mother's Day

By Katharina More

My mom is the best
(one of the best)
the greatest mom
happy things she does
excellent
mom
really
special.

Katharina More, Rahe, Germany. Christmas, 2001.

On Holy Ground

By Gerda Taylor

When I think about my mother I visualize her when she was much younger. She was a beautiful woman who always smiled, especially when she returned from her work as a midwife. She would say, "We had a little boy today!" or "We had a little girl today!" or "Everything went well—mother and child are doing fine!"

I would often watch her as she rode her bike on the way to making her six or seven visits to the families who had just been blessed with a newborn baby. She would take care of mother and child until the mother was able to care for the baby on her own.

Her starched white cap and black veil, which covered most of her beautiful hair, would fly in the wind as she rode away on her bicycle. What joy my mother must have felt each time she held a newborn in her hands! Indeed, how many babies did she help into this world? I don't know the total; I only know that she was very popular. Families called from far away to ask her to be their midwife.

This took place in the 1950s, when many mothers chose a midwife in order to have their child born in the privacy and comfort of their homes. I was six years old when my mother started her career and I was fascinated when I watched her sterilize her instruments and powder her rubber gloves. She was always ready for the next phone call that took her to yet another family awaiting a child! Often the homes were many kilometers away, and the road would lead her into the darkness until, in the distance, she would spot the home by seeing a dim light. An anxious father was usually outside, waiting.

I remember that most babies were born in the night. My mother, however, always managed to get home to prepare breakfast for me before school.

When a problem with her leg prevented her from continuing with her career, she was heartbroken. She had such love for her work. Life was no longer the same for her when she gave up her work as midwife.

When I was in school, my mom always encouraged me to go on trips with the other students. Even when I made the decision to follow my dream and travel to the United States, she supported me—she thought it would be a good idea for me to learn new things and become more independent. Of course, she thought I would return after a year. She was with me when I stepped onto that plane that took me thousands of miles away from her and that small town in northern Germany. Her smiles and encouragement went with me as she waved good-bye.

Years have passed and my mother lives by herself. She is eighty-three years old now, has osteoporosis and continues to have a lot of trouble with an ulcerous leg. My brother lives nearby, visits her every day, and brings her everything she needs, including meals. I visit as often as I am able, approximately every three years. When I first arrive during those visits, I realize how much she has aged. I now think much differently about leaving a mother behind. Her age has changed her very much. She pays no attention to the fact that hot water, a warm room, and occasional repairs to her home are necessary. This is very disturbing to my brother and myself. I've written many letters to her throughout the thirty-some years I've lived in America. She is no longer able to answer my letters, nor can she see enough to read them.

I have a beautiful picture of my mother. She is sitting in a lawn chair enjoying the sunshine, surrounded by our many flowers. I will always keep this picture of her youth and beauty in my heart. I draw strength from her and remember the things she taught me. My daily prayers begin with her. One of them goes as follows: *"Dear God, please let me see her one more time. Watch over her until I can be with her once again. Amen."*

One year later

Once again God's miracles became known to me during the planning of my sudden trip to Germany, as well as during the first week of my stay in my hometown. God is in control—not I! During my daily visits with mother at the hospital, it occurred to me that her life didn't seem to have any meaning any longer. I became painfully aware that there was no quality to her life: no sight, difficulty in hearing, conversation limited to nurses, the only visitors (before I came) my brother, or my niece. She was pretty much helpless.

2 Corinthians 5:16 warns us to "regard no one from a worldly point of view." Elsewhere we are reminded that "inwardly we are being renewed day by day." My mother was being renewed daily. I sat by an open window that day and cried many tears—through which I prayed to God for my mom, myself, and anyone I felt needed prayer that moment. As my tears flowed freely, I became very calm and without fear. Later that day I asked myself, did my tears flow to release all my

anxieties about my mother's possible death, or to make me understand that some of my prayers were being answered, or was I simply to learn that my mom was in fact aware of my presence and glad to have me there?

I had suddenly wondered if she even cared! How selfish of me, to be struggling with those, my own feelings! The time God had given me was meant for my mom—without any reservation. At that moment I once more bowed down in prayer and thanked my God for giving me this quality time with my mother.

I held her hand, braided her hair, touched her face often and spoke to her softly. Later, during the two weeks of her hospital stay, a very young pastor showed up. He told me his name was Dominique and he was assigned to this particular hospital. He was unbelievably calm when he spoke in Low German to my mom. He asked her some simple questions, and she understood him. Then he made the cross on her forehead and said the *Das Vater Unser* (The Lord's Prayer). She told him that she felt the blessing. I believe that from that moment on, my mother relaxed and "gave up."

She became very weak, and we brought her to a beautiful nursing home. Her weakness continued and she developed pneumonia on one side. Her breathing became very difficult.

I had to go back to the United States. The morning before my trip I went to see her and found her sleeping still at 9:00 AM. She was slowly slipping into deep sleep. I was back in my own home in Illinois and in the process of getting my life reorganized when the call from my brother came. My mother had passed away that evening.

Sometime during my stay in Germany my brother took down my confirmation certificate. It had been hanging in my old room for some years. "Take it home," he said. The scripture reads, *Dennoch bleibe ich stets by Dir; denn Du haelts mich bei meiner rechten Hand* (Psalm 73, verse 23): "Yet I am always with you; you hold me by my right hand." I used this scripture when preparing for my mother's funeral.

God is always with us. What a comfort to know this!

The Chimney

By Willie Fokkena

I saw a chimney, perched on a steep roof,
Stark and alone; I wondered if that chimney
Even had some friends.
It seems so independent and strong once.
No one could harm it.
But the moss at its base and the
Soot at its guts
Are slowly starting to break it up.
And it seems fragile, perilously perched out
At an angle.
Alone but no longer strong,
It shouldn't have been so independent.

I've got something to tell
I've got something to show
But it's gonna take a while
It's gonna take a while

I've got something to give
I've got something to find
But it's gonna take a while
It's gonna take a while

I've got friends in my life
Friends, who know what I mean
And I hope they're gonna stay a while
They're gonna stay a while

And maybe, someday there's you
Yes maybe, someday there's you
And I hope you're gonna stay a while
You're gonna stay a while

~Jens Pfeifer

The Dictionary Definition of 'Eulogy' Is 'High Praise'

By Laura Fokkena

He was actually my aunt's husband's brother-in-law, which made him an uncle of sorts. That's how my family works.

Two summers ago I found out he was seventy. He mentioned the age of his son and I asked how that was possible. Was he five years old when he had children? No, he said, and he was older than I thought: seventy that summer, and thereafter my conceptualization of what it means to be seventy was permanently altered. Seventy is cool. I can't wait until I'm seventy.

When I'm seventy I will drink wine with my meals and tell you of the time I met a man who saw Napoleon. "When I was little"—I will tell you—"I went to a parade with my father. And my father pointed to that man, that elderly gentleman, and my father said 'that man saw Napoleon in a field when he was five years old. That old man was once young, too, and when he was young he climbed to the top of a tree, as children do, and watched as Napoleon himself went into battle.'" I will tell you this.

When I'm seventy I'll travel to Iowa, sit on a picnic bench, and listen to my niece read her poorly written essays. She'll be shy and embarrassed but my wife will refer to her as "the author," which will, unbeknownst to me, give her the confidence to send her unsolicited manuscripts to publishers for the first time in years. My niece will achieve her first book credit in this manner.

A year later I will ask her what she's working on ("written your novel yet?") as though I take her seriously, and she will respond with "four things, actually," as though she takes herself seriously, too.

◆　　　◆　　　◆

Back when this niece was eleven she'll have visited me in Minneapolis. My wife will have introduced her to the game of Twenty Questions, which she'll play with her German cousins. It will take nineteen yes or no questions for her to real-ize she has to guess the name of a dead man—a dead man! how many millions of men have died before her?—and she'll say, for lack of better options, knowing she's beat, "I dunno…. George Washington?"

"*Right!!*" my wife will exclaim, pointing at her across the broad wooden table, and it will serve as a moment of triumph for her small self for years to come, a moment so fantastic she'll remember it still, more than twenty years later. George Washington, the prototypical dead man.

We'll play another game that summer, a quiz I picked up from work, one that attempts to find the words hidden in common initials, such as 1,001 A.N.—*1,001 Arabian Nights*—or 3 B.M. (S.H.T.R.)—*3 blind mice (see how they run)*. My niece is intrigued with this game, not because it holds any inherent fas-cination, but because she is capable of participating in something with which real, live adults concern themselves, however offhandedly. While their conversa-tion moves on to other topics she furrows her brow and sets herself to decipher-ing these puzzles, wanting to prove herself worthy. By the end of the weekend only a few obstinate phrases remain unsolved.

Several months later the quiz will be long forgotten, until she gets an unmarked letter in the mail: unsigned, with no return address, postmarked from St. Paul. Who does she know in St. Paul? No one. The only personal mail she gets is from her grandparents in Germany, but they're in Clarksville right now and they don't send her letters. And of course her pen pal, Kristie, the soccer goalie, but Kristie lives in Missouri. Who would be writing her from St. Paul?

She opens the letter.

"*200 dollars for passing go in Monopoly,*" the note will read.

That's it. No signature, no explanation.

200 dollars for passing go in Monopoly?

My niece will remain puzzled for several days. But as she tells her mother about the mysterious letter—at the drive-in restaurant on the outskirts of Clarks-ville—it will suddenly come to her. As I knew it would.

"Oh my gosh!" she'll almost shout, then quickly clamp her hand over her mouth. And then, by way of explanation: "Two hundred dollars for passing go in Monopoly! *200 D. for P.G. in M.!*"

My niece's mother will still be confused, but no matter. My niece under-stands. She remembers. She remembers even now, at age thirty: remembers every time she plays Monopoly with her own daughter. *200 D. for P.G. in M.* She rounds the corner with her shoe or hat or thimble, past Park Place, past Boardwalk, always wanting to explain as she collects her stash, but knowing that it's too much detail, too tangential to the game. But she'll tell her daughter someday.

200 D. for P.G. in M., she'll relate. *Two hundred dollars for passing go in Monopoly.*

The letter's real intent? *I remember that you were interested.* It's because of experiences like this that she'll ask nine-year-old Katherine at the afterschool program where she works to write about her trip to the Dominican Republic, or seek out Brian and tell him something she read about ancient Rome the other day. "I've been meaning to tell you…" she'll say, catching them on the stairwell. They give her quizzical looks, not used to being the focus of attention unless they're in trouble, but they come to her later with questions, with articles clipped out of *National Geographic*, with the stories they've handwritten with colored pencils on wide-ruled notebook paper.

I remember that you were interested.

◆   ◆   ◆

When I'm seventy I'll invite this niece and her seven-year-old daughter to my antique farm in Maine. Late at night she'll call me from a cell phone on an abandoned road in Dresden, telling me she's lost. I'll find her across the street from the clapboard church and lead her through the winding gravel roads flanked on either side by rock walls—this portion of Maine is drowning in rock, which is bad for farmers but good for stoneworkers—past the blueberry patch and up the hill to the old house, where I'll give them a bed under a handmade quilt and a sloping rooftop. From this room she can hear nothing but the wind and the bark of a Brittany spaniel named Mitch, who looks and feels exactly like the dog she had as a child. Mitch is old, and blind, and he bumps into things. It's hard to watch, such aging.

The next day I'll drive them to the state house in Augusta, to the old jail in Wiscasset (imprisoning the populace since 1811!), to Pemaquid Point Lighthouse, where we'll sit against the ocean, smelling the salt and comforting the seven-year-old who's convinced she's about to fall through the cracks in the rocks and be abandoned to the Atlantic for eternity. The lawn behind us will be blocked off unexpectedly, and we'll wonder why until we see a woman in a bridal gown emerge from behind the lighthouse and realize we are accidental witnesses to a wedding. We'll eat seafood and drive home past rowhouses and I'll talk about growing up in Lowell and she'll talk about moving to Boston and we'll exchange stories of triple-deckers, foreign to both of us now: foreign to me because they're a part of my past, foreign to her because she's new to them. New England will suddenly be exotic all over again.

At dinner that night I'll tell her that I grew up with Jack Kerouac; I'll tell her that it's true he played ball in high school, *"but, you know, we all did."*

More than that I'll tell her of Edwin Arlington Robinson, my uncle (of sorts), even though she admits she only knows of Richard Cory from a Paul Simon song. I'll tell her of the real Richard Cory, Edwin's brother Dean, who was addicted to morphine: a family secret; historians write him off as a run-of-the-mill alcoholic. I'll take her to his birthplace in Head Tide and his gravesite in Gardiner, explain to her the connection between the poet and this house she's staying in, the one with the quilt and the sloping rooftop, built by the poet's aunt and uncle, who are also my great-great-grandparents. She won't be good at remembering the chain of ancestry (she's bad like that), but she'll remember the stories of young Edwin spending his summers in this house, remember that he was expected to help with the work but being a poet he was more the read-by-the-haystack sort, and that this was a source of irritation with the rest of the family.

My wife will take her down to the basement and tell her that they used to go out in the dead of winter and pour water in the crevices of boulders. At night the water would freeze and crack the stones in two, an ear-splitting sound she's only read about in *Laura Ingalls*. The next morning they'd go and collect those split rocks and use them to build their basement, an endeavor my niece will think about employing if she ever builds a house herself.

I'll tell her of my great-grandfather's journal that I found on the property. He was a carriage repairman in the 1800s who dutifully recorded every one of his business transactions. One young lad, "Moses," made frequent appearances at the carriage shop (and thus in the journal), to the point where I began to wonder about the level of my great-grandfather's craftsmanship—why was Moses' carriage always falling apart? The mystery is solved deeper in the diary, when my great-grandfather mentions, with typical lack of emotion, that his daughter married Moses that day. I'll chuckle at the thought of clever Moses purposefully breaking his carriage wheels so that he'd have an excuse to limp back up to the carriage house and get a glimpse of the repairman's daughter.

The next day my niece will wander into the forest behind my house and find me doing repair work of my own, on slim slabs of stone dating back to the 1700s that I've carefully maintained, almost against the law—"after the Civil War it was illegal to bury people outside of cemeteries"—and I'll share with her the life histories of each person buried below, including the speculation that one of them might have come all the way from India, what with a name like that. She'll be reminded that I'm an engineer by trade as she sees me wrapping bands across the tombstones and molding them back into place, keeping them upright even as time and weather battle against my efforts.

One year later, almost to the day, they'll cremate me and inter my remains here in this family cemetery, and I'll think it's only fitting. On the day I die my niece will be working on her oral history class, explaining to inner city eight-year-olds the importance of their lives and of their memories, and continually reminding them that even ordinary people have stories to tell.

◆ ◆ ◆

That same Minneapolis summer, the summer of German cousins, the Twenty Questions summer, the *200 D. for P.G. in M.* summer, she'll take her mother aside after they set up their sleeping bags in my living room and whisper: *"Why does he talk like that?"*

"He's from Massachusetts," her mother will whisper back, and that will be that.

My niece won't recall that exchange for twenty years, until she moves to Massachusetts herself and hears me all the time, in the accents of her neighbors and co-workers. A week after my funeral she'll be driving through southern Illinois in the middle of night, her daughter sleeping in the backseat. And—as though he's speaking to her personally—the overnight DJ from public radio will do a story on the sale of Jack Kerouac's manuscript. She'll remember my wife telling her about this, remember the concerns about the price and whether or not the scroll will be displayed in a museum or in a private residence.

And then she'll hear someone reading from *On the Road*, and for a moment, just a moment, she'll wonder who it is, who's reading Kerouac's words here, at three a.m., sliding through the cornfields of southern Illinois.

But then there it is—*my* voice, clear and clean and crisp, speaking to her through that unmistakable Lowell accent, and she'll know immediately that it's authentic: this is Kerouac himself, dropping his r's and spinning schwas all over his vowels. (*"Why does he talk like that?"*)

It's for her benefit, hers alone, that Kerouac reads. It's been said that anyone can make Paris exotic, but Jack Kerouac was the only one who could do the same thing for Topeka. She begs to differ. Much as she loves Kerouac, she knows that I, too, could create grandeur out of anything.

Her car slips through the dark of midwestern America. Her daughter sleeps, the trees heave along the roadside, the barns veer on the edge of collapse, and *she is not alone.* I'm watching her, via the satellites of public radio, and she knows with certainty only one thing, and that is this: if she makes to seventy, she'll emulate me as best she can so that her grandchildren (of sorts) can have something approximating my influence in their lives.

She'll give them a bed under a handmade quilt and tell them she knew someone who grew up with Jack Kerouac, that she knew someone who was related to the real Richard Cory. That she knew someone who knew someone who climbed a tree and saw Napoleon. She'll ask her grandchildren what they're working on, and when they say "four things, actually," she'll serve them wine and take them seriously.

His words were magic and his heart was true,
And everywhere he wandered he was blessed.
Out of all ancient men my childhood knew
I choose him and I mark him for the best.

~Edwin Arlington Robinson, "Uncle Ananias"

Coming To Terms

By Connor Durflinger

I feel as though I've gotten to know the city better today. Boston was merciful and cooler, and although I do not have the illusion that the city cares for me, I have learned to appreciate how deep it is, in its rough beauty.

We have had this adversarial relationship, the city and I, because I could never really see the essence of it. All I saw was this part of State Street and downtown here and there, that part of Dorchester where I lived, and a lot of trips up 93 and down 128. Downtown was an obstacle, the thing that kept me from home for two hours in the sweltering heat while I inched down the Central Artery.

I went into today not expecting much of it, as I was tired and wasted from the torrid excess of the last couple of days. I dragged my ass into the office, nauseous and dehydrated and beaten down by city.

The office was dead, and Dom, my boss, wound up inviting me and the two other engineers, Jon and Greg, to go out on his boat for the afternoon. I didn't really expect much of that going into it, either. It turned out to be fabulous. I could have stood in the bow of that boat for hours as it cut from wave to wave. There was fairly high water today, with 15-25mph winds, but the boat just knew what to do as it sliced through each crest.

The sight of the whole coastline of the bay, from Marblehead down to Quincy, was touristy-gushingly awe-inspiring. We tooled around the bay for a while, as Dom needed to get gas for the boat, which is this total ordeal of finding the right path between the red and green buoys. Dom is this great guy, a blunt and compact man with a wide, expressive Italian manner. Totally unpretentious.

Being out on the water with those guys was good, just genuinely good in that uncomplicated way that I rarely find with other men. "I always make a fuckin' idiot of myself when I go to fuckin' get gas," Dom shouts to us over the engine, regaling us with stories about how he'd dropped his keys overboard (to be retrieved later by a scuba diver), tossed his boathook overboard for no good reason (only to have it wash up on the dock as he pulled in), and rammed the dock with his boat.

"See over there? That's Egg Rock. They call it that 'cos all the fuckin' birds shit all over the top, so it's totally fuckin' white. For real, look at the fuckin' thing. See right by it? That's where Keefe fuckin' grounded his boat on the rocks tryin' to take a fuckin' shortcut. Always tryin' to take a fuckin' shortcut he is. I look like a fuckin' idiot every time I get gas over here, but I'm man enough not to be afraid of bein' a fool.

"I brought a girl out here on the boat last night and she wound up fuckin' puking over the side. *Awwww, shit, babe*, I said. I can see I'm not gonna have a fuckin' goodnight kiss, huh?"

I like Dom.

Greg and I cut up like class clowns in the back of the boat. We were both wearing our office mufti, of course, since we'd both wussed out on wearing shorts into the office. The whole ride down Greg had been playing CDs of his old bands, really good stuff, and he was recapturing his twenties.

After the ride was over, Greg and I headed back to the office and smoked up. Greg is the guy who'll always smoke you up, very cool in a geeky-musician-nebbish kind of way. He dropped me off at the T, muttering about how he was going to catch hell from his wife when he got home.

I looked pretty frightful with salt caked on my slacks and whatnot, but I was elated. I felt like I *got* it, that I finally understood something about why people want to live here, that the nautical motifs on the walls of buildings really did mean something and it wasn't just all about expensive yachts as toys for the rich.

Riding the T home, something made me get off at Haymarket. I'd heard about the fabulous stuff down here, but had never really explored. I was totally entranced by the bustle of a Friday night and the open stalls and markets. I rounded a corner and found myself walking on cobblestones.

The geographical center of Boston really *is* the heart of the city—the Financial District, Quincy Marketplace, Faneuil Hall, Downtown Crossing. Walking along, say, Boylston Street from Back Bay, then down the Freedom Trail in reverse. You can feel the modern city peeling away; the sediment of habitation accumulates more thickly.

First you move out of the part of the city that was built up from the harbor; landfill reclaiming the sea. You cross from the great green space of Boston Common and the Public Gardens, and the too-modern Prudential Building disappears behind trees and brownstones. Down Tremont, into Downtown Crossing. Traffic disappears and there are only pedestrians, spilling out onto the brick streets. And the crowd in Boston! The folks in the skyscrapers may still be mainly white, but the scene on the ground is diverse as hell.

As you walk down Washington up the Freedom Trail, the Macy's and the Filene's vanish behind you; ahead, the Old State House (1711). Put your back to the last of the skyscrapers, put your back to the gold-leafed Fleet Center and cross State and pass down an alley where the names of the workers who built it are etched into the building.

Find yourself at the edge of the old waterfront, Quincy Market and Faneuil Hall (1742). It's a warm day and the people are just hanging. Nobody's in much of a hurry, as downtown has largely emptied out; there's a game at Fenway Park later. Across from the vile City Hall (which looks like a team of left-brain injured primates were given the job of drafting a warm and welcoming civic center in the style of New Soviet Realism crossed with a Mayan temple complex, but I digress) you find Faneuil Hall positively fucking inspiring in a no-bullshit kind of way.

I mean, you could have seen Tom Paine preaching revolt against the king and radical democracy right out that window. You could have seen that moment and been one of the ones to *first* say that it's fucking self-evident that all people are created equal. End of story because we're fucking *earnest* about it to the point of carrying out midnight raids on ships and revolting against the Divine Right of Kings and so on.

Now you work your way deeper in and walk up the cobblestoned, pedestrian-only roads into the center of town, and it *is* just a town. It's like finding the medulla oblongata, the lizard brain of the city. The John Hancock house is there with a little clutch of restaurants and shops, twisted sclerotic pathways joining them. There are old, raw emotions here, and you can look beyond the gift shop and see the real fucking *root* of society.

They called Boston "The Hub of the Universe" then, and its inhabitants termed "brahmins," and how could you *not* feel like Masters Of The Fucking Universe after you rebirthed a political form dead for 2,000 years in the West. Kicked out the British Empire. With plenty of the raw nation spreading off the map in all directions, we were seemingly complete and self-sufficent. You wonder if Paine or Paul Revere or John Adams ever just stopped and said, 'This is pretty fucked up, right here."

I let myself get swept up in that imagining, and I rounded a corner and saw an intersection that I swear to sweet Jesus I have seen before in a dream. As I walked by the open windows and doors of a Haymarket pub, "Landslide" came pouring out. Some cover band, really good. I was totally in a rush and called Laura on the spot to ramble on about it.

I hung out there for a while, transfixed. In my day today, I'd been from Dorchester, into South Boston and taken the T up to Everett. Then up to

Swampscott, out into the harbor. Back down to downtown, all the way here into the still-vital marrow. I let myself get seduced by the notion of a city that is so historically democratic and activist, a city that steamed with revolutionary ambition. I stood there with the sea-salt crusted in my beard and let The Hub of the Universe spin about me as I sat on my bench, chatting with an Indonesian man. He'd first been to America last September 10.

We both sat and smoked in silence for a bit. He spoke of his daughter, of Las Vegas, wafting clove smoke at me. I gestured widely at Faneuil Hall, said something about the real urge for democracy here. How we should do better, not necessarily more, abroad. He complained about the state of his government, the economy. I ate a hot Italian sausage bought from a Polish vendor who argued loudly in bad Spanish with the Dominicans who were giving her a hard time about the onions.

The city has been generous to me today, and although I still do not think it cares about me as such, I respect what it is, the first steps in a huge unfinished human project. (No, not the Big Dig. Democracy.) And when the black dudes who rolled up on me, one talking quickly and hey can you hear this out see here's what we're trying to do just a DOLLAR, man—HEY CUZ GET BACK HERE—and just like a DOLLAR or so—

I stop long enough for respect but push off with a "folks, I'm late, good luck to ya" before his cousin catches up with him to swing into good cop/bad cop and I'm back on the subway. Back through time to Dorchester, Savin Hill, ironically the oldest of it all. The former cow-track that is Pleasant Street (1620) curves past our window, and I want to feel it again. Like you really *can* overthrow the king.

East Meets West

By Christian Brandenburg

[Johann and Hilda Fokkena's granddaughter Ute Brost was born in Williamsport, Pennsylvania, and moved to Germany when she was three years old. She was raised in Oldenburg and went to university in Hannover, where she met Christian Branden-burg shortly after the Berlin Wall fell. They were married in Germany and now live in Cedar Falls, Iowa, with their two daughters, Charlotte and Mathilde. We asked Christian to tell us about growing up in East Germany and the changes he experienced after moving to America.]

I was born in Stralsund, a small town on the Baltic Sea in northeast Germany. It's a very pretty and very old town. My parents are both teachers. My mother taught piano at a music school in Germany and my father taught violin there.

I have a sister who is five years younger than I am. When we were growing up, we were very lucky to live in a small row house from the 1930s which my great-grandfather had built himself. My grandparents on my father's side had an apart-ment around the block on the next street so I saw them quite frequently. My other grandparents lived in Hameln, in Lower Saxony. They moved there when I was five, just before my sister was born.

We are going back to Stralsund in two weeks. It is a small medieval town. There is a wonderful island and there is one highway going to the island. When I was growing up, my parents had the same vacations that we had, so we would spend any halfway sunny day on the beach. It's a forty-five minute drive. There are even chalky beaches. We drove there a lot. It's usually too mild to snow. Most winters are around thirty degrees with slush and sleet. The summers are mild, so we never shut off the heater completely. The latitude is about the same as Ost-friesland.

Even though it was difficult for younger people to get out of East Germany, retirees could leave very easily. My grandparents decided to leave and they came to visit us two or three times a year for a week or ten days at a time.

Since my parents were both music teachers, they would do quite a bit of prac-ticing and sometimes rehearsed chamber music when I was small. I remember sit-ting under the grand piano occasionally when they practiced. I was always around classical music, and when I was in second grade I started violin lessons at the music school. My father was my teacher. The instrument teachers would go and visit the public schools and give them music instruction and try to see who showed a strong interest in music or who had a talent. They would approach the families and ask if they were interested in pursuing music. Since my parents were both music teachers, I didn't really have a choice. At first I didn't want to, but I got talked into it and never regretted it.

Later on students could get up to ninety minutes of lesson time, and it was free or had a small fee. These schools still exist in Germany with a state subsidy to keep the schools going. There was a special public school in Berlin which also provided a lot of music instruction. You had to audition on your instrument to get in and you also had to have a good grade average. The school had a tight schedule with a day off in the middle of the week. There was school on Saturday to keep everybody busy. The school was to prepare students for the music conser-vatory. That school still exists and has been turned into a music gymnasium. It is a very small school with a lot of additional music instruction.

Since I was playing violin, I had to have piano lessons once a week. We had music theory and many conservatory courses so we could finish some courses that were required at the conservatory. You were supposed to practice your instru-ment at least three or four hours a day.

The first two years I lived in the boarding house that was attached to the school. It was supported by the government, and once you were admitted, every-thing was taken care of. You had to share your room with two other people, and the food was very awful.

I was fourteen when I went there. I was going into ninth grade, and I had three years to go there. It was a fun time and I don't regret it. I went home every Saturday after school. It was a four hour train ride each way. We would go back to the boarding house on Sunday night after dark.

After finishing a couple of years at the conservatory in Berlin, I moved to Han-nover to finish music at the Hochschule for music and theater in Hannover. I moved in the fall of 1990, so Ute and I met in the spring of 1991. We had a mutual friend. Ute's best friend Katharina was in my violin class. Ute went to a recital to see Katharina play, and I was there. Ute and I first met there. We sat by each other at dinner after the recital. We met at Katharina's house a couple of times, and we went to see "Dances with Wolves" with a bunch of friends. We sat next to each other.

Later I went to see my grandmother. I told her about Ute. I didn't know she was American yet. My grandmother told me later that she knew I was in love.

East and West

Were there differences in our backgrounds because of the wall? There were differences, but since I had my grandparents in West Germany, as long as I can remember there was always a lot of connection to that side even though we couldn't go there. In 1982 my grandfather was seventy-five, and they signed up with a European human rights organization which allowed some people with immediate family in West Germany to go there sometimes.

It was very difficult. You had to do all sorts of paperwork and you had a secret service check that you didn't know about until your neighbors, your employers, and your colleagues were asked about you. The government was always very concerned about people coming back. I remember my mom being able to go to visit my grandfather for his seventy-fifth birthday. It was fine. She could even go in the middle of the school year. Nobody cared. She just had to be back on time. If she had come back even a day late, the whole family would have been in huge trouble and would probably never have been able to go again. From that point on I think she was able to go once every year.

A few years later, around 1986 or 1987, they loosened the restrictions a little bit more and allowed people to visit aunts and uncles. My father had an uncle in Düsseldorf, and even though they had absolutely no contact, he visited him for a few days, and then for the rest of the days he went to visit my grandparents. He did that once each winter.

There was an orchestra during the school year and someone organized young string players to get together at a camp for a week and rehearse every day for about six hours. Then there was a concert. I was able to meet a lot of people that way. The conductors and people who rehearsed the sectionals were professionals. It was somewhere around Berlin usually. I was introduced to professional musicians. Those musicians were on tour throughout the world and had seen things behind the curtain. That was an encouragement. It was my main encouragement to actually study and to get one of those jobs and to be able to go and see the other side of the curtain. I wanted to get one of those jobs, go on a tour, and not come home. My parents knew about that. They encouraged us to do it. They felt they had missed the chance and they encouraged us to go that route. It was extremely tough because if I had done this, I would never have been able to go back home. My parents would never have been allowed to leave until they were retired. That is probably the price that we would have paid. A lot of people did that. The orchestra leaders figured that about 96 or 97 people came back out of every 100 who went on the tour.

That was common knowledge. In order to be able to travel as a musician, I would have had to have the job for a couple of years and after a while they would allow you to participate. All over the world it is typical for classical orchestras to travel and give concert tours.

One of those people I got to know from the school is my sister's father-in-law. It is a small world. I remember very well when I was twelve or thirteen he showed us slide shows about Japan. I remember him telling that if there was a concert tour to Japan, they would take a whole suitcase full of food so they wouldn't have to spend their hard currency on food. They would buy TVs and stuff like that. They would have a whole container shipped back of things people had bought that wouldn't fit in the airplane.

I remember him always complaining and not being happy about having a tour that included the U.S., especially if the U.S. was on the tour first, because you couldn't bring any food. That impressed me very much, and I think it influenced me more than I was aware of at the time.

German reunification

As soon as the wall came down, I quit school in Berlin and a couple of months later I started up in Hannover but then after a while I kind of realized that the original motivation to be a musician wasn't there. It was taken care of.

The arts funding went downhill in Germany. I suppose you can't just keep printing money. East Germany didn't really have a functional economy. If they needed money, they printed money to pay people. People had lots of money in the bank and there was nothing to buy with the money at the stores. If you wanted to buy a car, you were on a waiting list for ten or fifteen years. By that time, you had the money saved up to buy three cars, but you couldn't do it. There was a booming black market where people would buy things like cars. After the ten- or fifteen-year waiting period was up, they could sell it for three or four times as much money to somebody else because there was so much money floating around and there was nothing to buy with it.

In West Germany everything was paid by the government and financed through very high tax rates. The tax rates in Germany these days are so high that there is no way you can even think about raising any more public money. I have heard the arts and public schools are not doing very well.

In East Germany there was too much of everything. Every little city had an opera house and not a lot to do some of the time. It's tough, but I think it had to be reduced and especially in Berlin because it was a divided city and they had everything twice. Everything was double. They are still struggling to simplify things and unify things. Nobody likes it. My sister is a victim of it. After years of auditioning she got a job, and I think after two or three years they are closing down her orchestra. They don't have enough money to keep it going. My brother-in-law is a musician and has a good job, but in the last five or six years they have had their incomes cut instead of raised. I think they have had at least a ten percent reduction in pay. They still have enough pay, but that's the trend, and it's probably going to continue that way for quite a while.

They have to cut incomes or eliminate jobs. Anywhere in the European Union is open to anybody from the E.U. In a few years everyone may be fighting for the same jobs. Since Germany is a high wage country, there will be enormous competition for these jobs. The Germans are not at all willing to relocate. Taking a job in Denmark or Holland is unheard of to most people. They would rather collect unemployment benefits than move from one end of Germany to another. That isn't true of everyone, of course. It is a strange side effect of an overly generous welfare system.

There are some jobs for musicians, but some jobs will be eliminated. As my parents and others retire, their jobs will be eliminated. They offered public employees early retirement packages which are attractive. Those jobs will be turned into positions that paid by the hour.

Supporting the arts

How do I feel about state-supported arts compared to their every-man-for-himself counterparts? I wish there would be a middle ground. The state-sponsored way is not the best way because the arts programs are so totally dependent on tax revenue, and there are times when that isn't enough. Everybody complains, but no one does anything. When the tax rates are very high as they are in Germany, it is almost impossible to convince wealthy people to give away any money or for corporations to sponsor the arts because they often pay fifty percent of their profit in taxes already.

There is very little encouragement to give any significant amount of money to a good cause. I feel like the way the arts are funded in Waterloo and Cedar Falls is working fairly well. It is funded from mostly private sources. Artists need to be working harder to provide what people want to hear or see rather than just doing what the conductor wants to do.

I remember one story from a friend in Germany who has an orchestra job. She works at a little opera house. There was an opera on the schedule and hardly anyone ever showed up. They knew that from the start, and they did it anyway even though it was funded by public tax money. What I see here in Iowa with the orchestras, the museums, and the arts is public support. There are many wealthy people who see it as their duty and an honor to give significant amounts of money to the arts including the theater. I think it makes people more appreciative of what they have if they have to fight for it and if they have to work harder to raise the money. They are more aware and more proud of what they have in the community. They feel more connected to it.

Moving to America

When we were students, we took a four week vacation in the spring of 1992 to visit here in the States. There was a Brost family reunion when Ray turned sixty. I remember Habbo gave us a huge old green van, and we drove off all the way to Arizona and to California and back. We slept in the van every other day, and we slept in a proper bed the days in between. Because of that and the idea that I didn't want to make a living being a musician, it was my idea to move here. I also found out it would be extremely difficult to learn violin-making in Germany because I had already graduated from college. Higher education is free in Germany, but you are restricted to one profession. It would have been very difficult to get into a completely different field in Germany. It would have been difficult to learn it as an apprentice because no one wants to train a competitor.

Ray researched it and found out about the school for violin-making in Salt Lake City. He contacted them. It was the fall of 1992. Ute had a childhood friend who was kind of a self-taught violin-maker in Ostfriesland. I spent time with her and became motivated to learn to make violins, and she helped me prepare a piece so I wouldn't have to go to Salt Lake City to take an entrance exam.

I didn't speak any English in 1992. It was very frustrating because most Americans don't speak a second language. They speak louder or slower instead of using simpler sentences or different words. We moved here in the summer of '93 because I started in the school at Salt Lake City in the fall.

I think we are going to stay here forever. I became a citizen four years ago. It's always in the back of your mind to perhaps move back someday, but it's very unlikely I think. It's especially unlikely that we would go back to Germany. The mentality is different. Last time I was back was different. It was home, but it was not. It was strange.

Certainly as long as the children are in school, I don't think we are going to go anywhere. Cedar Falls seems to be a nice place to raise kids and they have a good public school system. There are hardly any problems. Nobody ever gets shot here.

First impressions of America

America was open space. Even in '92 I remember Habbo picking us up in Minneapolis and just having all this open space with no people. It is something that is very difficult to find in Germany. It's a different life. It's an easier life. People are less concerned about appearances, especially in the country such as around Clarksville. People can drive around in pickup trucks that have more holes than metal. That is something no one would ever dare to do in Germany. They would just be embarrassed by what others would think, not to mention that the safety inspectors would junk it.

It's open space. I remember driving west. We had never been in Utah. It was an adventure. We had two cars and a trailer. I think it was halfway through Wyoming that one of the cars quit. It was a little problem, but it got me worked up. It didn't want to go up the hill with the heavy load in the back, but it made it to the next gas station and was fixed.

All this space, and the mountains! I still remember that first impression when we entered the Rockies. I can't find the word for it. It was overwhelming having these humongous mountains and nobody living in most of that space. One thing I miss in Iowa is the mountains. If we ever move away from Iowa, I would want to have real mountains or the ocean. I'd want the mountains even more than the water. It was just impressive scenery, such as those canyons where the highways go through.

It was rather strange going to Salt Lake City. It was a place we had never been, and we didn't know a soul, but this is supposed to be your home for a couple of years. At first we had a tiny little apartment right next to the school. We had a telephone we could use whenever we wanted and how often we wanted.

A couple of months later we moved into a bigger place on the wrong side of town, which we learned after we moved there. Ute tried to teach private lessons at home. We were not aware from Germany that there was a "right" and a "wrong" side of town to live in. It looked fine, but it was one street too far out of the preferred area. A lot of people wouldn't want to show up for lessons there. A few months later we moved again, and then we found the perfect place.

Raising children in the U.S.

We find it important to keep the German tradition and culture alive. Lotti was three years old before she started to speak any English. We spoke only German at home. She had her little friends, and they would talk at each other. They could play. They didn't have to understand anything. When she was three, we sent her to a preschool two days a week. During the first two weeks the teacher told us she didn't say a word, she just listened and observed and then she started to speak English.

Now that Lotti is in school, it is difficult to get her to switch back into German. We are stubborn. Since I work at home and don't have a lot of social life during the day, I never switch into English with the kids. Ute always tries to try to switch back into German. It's only the violin practicing that they do in English, because it would be too confusing if she has a teacher here at the Suzuki School and all the terms would have to be translated. Other than that we always speak German at home. We also bought a VCR that plays all the European videotapes so we have a whole shelf full of German children's videotapes.

We will make it a priority to go to Germany every couple of years, mainly for the kids. Mathilde will be two in six weeks. We are exposing her to only German at this point. As she gets older, we will have somebody introduce English to her, but there's no rush. They will pick it up easily. Now that Lotti has learned English, she has figured out how to read a German book.

Of course, I wish they could at some point spend more time in Germany. Perhaps they could go to school there for a year. That's something we dream about once in a while. We would like an exchange system where we could exchange jobs with a family for a year. They are too little to think about those things now.

How do our children's experiences contrast with mine? They are quite different. The whole political system is different. When I was little, growing up under Communism, the first thing we learned was not to repeat anything that was talked about at home. Don't repeat anything to someone we didn't know very well. When you would meet someone new, you would first want to know which side they were on politically. There was no legal opposition under Communism. Everybody who didn't agree just had to disagree quietly or with each other. You had to make sure that information didn't go out and be reported to someone who belonged to the Secret Service.

We had been indoctrinated very early to keep our mouths shut away from the house. I think our children have a very different experience. If they say in school that George Bush is an idiot, that's fine, but in East Germany it could have gotten your family in a lot of trouble. It could have gone so far that children could not attend the university as a reprimand for comments like that.

Last year Lotti went to the Montessori School and she goes to the Suzuki School. Next year she will go to the public school. My observations are that parents are more involved here in school. They are more involved in afterschool activities, rather than just dropping their children off and picking them up. I remember, as a young child of eight or nine, walking all across town to my orchestra lesson. I walked back even after dark, and it was perfectly normal. Now I can't imagine sending my young child off for a fifteen- or twenty-minute walk across town.

What do I hope for my children? I hope they keep up the connection to Germany and perhaps, since they are going to be bilingual, I hope that may be a significant advantage in certain career opportunities. I hope they travel back and forth. I hope they don't get caught up in thinking only about what's going on in this country and that everything in this country is perfect and everybody else doesn't count. I hope that they will get the message that that isn't true at all.

Thunderstorms in Osnabrück

By The Stammtisch Collective

Back when I was young, in the land of milk and honey
When I was just a kid, with coke and pocket money
When I was still a child, my bike upon the gravel
When I was still afraid, in the days before I traveled
I depended on my parents, who told me to obey
I depended on their judgment: right from wrong, I'd be ok
And I depended on my body, voice fading by the hour
But now I tell my daughter don't be scared to use your power

    But it doesn't matter now, cause I've got wine and I've got song
    I've got friends and close companions, though the road to here was long
    Now it's safe to tell the story, so come in and take a look
    We would all be at the table, but there's a storm in Osnabrück
    Mario, come join us, after the storm in Osnabrück

Remember the skyline of Chicago, the boats on the North Sea
Remember post cards, midnight phone calls, and our battle to be free
Remember roller skates and skateboards and our struggle to be bold
Remember your translations of the stories that I told
You bought your first guitar and then you taught yourself to sing
I bought a used typewriter and I started chronicling
A journey of our ancestors; you put my words to song
They almost lost their faith in us but I think we proved them wrong

    So it doesn't matter now, cause I've got wine and I've got song
    I've got friends and close companions and together we are strong
    Now it's safe to tell the story, come on in and take a look
    We'll all be at the table after storms in Osnabrück
    Mario will join us after storms in Osnabrück

As a girl I was chastised when I wandered from the script
I blamed myself, avoided risk, I hid inside my crypt
Now I'm grown and still denounced each time I stray outside the norm
But there's music in the air tonight and in Osnabrück a storm
So I will accept my fate and, yes, embrace my past
But I'll not follow blindly, nor do everything I'm asked
I'm balanced and I'm centered and my mind is full of wonder
The world is full of life and the skies are full of thunder

    Cause it doesn't matter now, for I've got wine and I've got luck
    I've got a table where they know me and a storm in Osnabrück
    I've got friends and close companions, results of chances that I took
    I made it here, so far so good, come on in and take a look
    Come in and take a look
    Mario after the thunderstorm
    Come on in and take a look

Four

By Heidi Sandler

The crowd thins outside, replaced with candle light
And, as the familiar faceless atmosphere
(is the dark responsible or the time?)
drops
like the brick of summer
onto
the
stoop,
and the small-town sounds
diminish one by one,
the spoken becomes the wondered
and wit becomes confession
most taboos broken
but the rifts repaired.

Home

By Willie Fokkena

You travel the whole world over
Lookin' for somethin' to see.
You come back home and discover
The goodness of simplicity.

Well, I've seen the Eiffel Tower
And beautiful beaches in Spain.
I've turned on to flower power,
Gotten high singing in the rain.
But I've never got that feeling
'Til I got home again.

About the Contributors

Dagmar Albers began her career as a teacher while living in Hildesheim, Germany, but after her husband's death she and her daughter Maike returned to Aurich to be near Dagmar's parents. There she has been a special education teacher for more than twenty years. A few years ago Maike joined the military, where she is training to become a doctor. Both Dagmar and Maike have traveled extensively, and Dagmar's art projects are coveted by envious family members.

Christian Brandenburg grew up in Germany and studied at the Musikhochschule Hannover. He and his wife, Ute (Brost), both accomplished musicians, moved to Salt Lake City, Utah, in 1993. Christian graduated from the Violin Making School of America in 1997, and now builds and restores string instruments. He and Ute live in Cedar Falls, Iowa, where they are raising their two daughters, Charlotte and Mathilde. Christian's expert restoration of their century-old "blue house with all the flowers" is well-admired by the neighborhood.

Gunda Brost grew up in Oldenburg, Germany, and speaks an unholy number of languages. A former Mrs. Nebraska, she earned a BA in French, Political Science, and Education from Wartburg College in Waverly, Iowa, as well as an MA in German from Middlebury College in Middlebury, Vermont. She is currently going to law school, teaching in Iowa, and raising her son, Benedict Bundi, whose father is from Tanzania in East Africa. Benedict has the distinction of being one of the very few first-born males in the lineage.

Ray Brost grew up in Medford, Wisconsin, and earned a BA from the University of Wisconsin-Madison as well as an MA in German Language and Literature from Middlebury College and Mainz University. He married Meta Fokkena in 1962 and, after spending a few years teaching in Williamsport, Pennsylvania, he moved to Germany, where he taught English and history at the Gymnasium Westerstede for twenty-five years. He and Meta returned to Iowa in 1993. Ray is currently building a house, by hand, out of stones he finds in old house and barn foundations. The work is slow-going, but if you mention that to him he will helpfully remind you that construction on the cathedral of Cologne began in 1248 and was not completed until 1880.

Connor Durflinger was born in Maryland and grew up in Kansas. He received a BA in Philosophy and History from Grinnell College in Grinnell, Iowa, and an MA in Philosophy from SUNY-Binghamton in New York. He works as a Systems Architect in Boston, Massachusetts, where he lives with Laura Fokkena, her daughter Rakaya, an idiosyncratic calico cat, and a Beta fish named Delta.

Rakaya El-Kasaby is the daughter of Laura Fokkena and Bassel El-Kasaby. She lives in Boston, Massachusetts, and loves computers, anime, and reading science fiction/fantasy novels. Rakaya plans to study wolves and help save them from extinction. She also thinks ferrets are cool.

Onno Fecht is the older son of Garrelt and Hinrike Fecht. He and his twin sister Gesa were born in their Tante Gerda's bedroom in Aurich, Germany. Onno grew up on his parents' farm in Rahe, and earned his Abitur from the Intergesamtschule in Aurich. Onno has studied law at the Universität Münster.

Habbo Fokkena was born in Walle, Germany, and moved to the United States at the age of nine. He received his law degree from the University of Iowa and had a private practice in Clarksville, Iowa, for twenty-five years before being appointed to United States Trustee for Iowa, Minnesota, North Dakota, and South Dakota in 2002. He lives on a farm outside Clarksville with his wife, Holly. A few years ago he got a new dog and, with all of his children out of the house, was allowed to name it Flockie.

Laura Fokkena grew up in Clarksville, Iowa, and received an MA in international development from the University of Iowa. She moved to Boston to co-found KITE, Inc., a nonprofit organization that donates computer equipment and other media tools to community development groups in the Third World. She spent three years working in the education area of a large urban after-school program in Boston, but recently switched to teaching English as a second language. Laura's understanding of Plattdeutsch, minimal as it may be, gives her the bizarre ability to understand entire passages in Yiddish and Afrikaans.

Lisa Fokkena was raised in Clarksville, Iowa. She has traveled to Europe several times, but also by car to every state in the contiguous U.S. with the arbitrary exception of Delaware. Lisa lives in Alaska now, where she is working in the tourism industry. She plans to continue her travels as well as help others get their one free hammer in life. She has hers already.

Willie Fokkena was born in Walle, Germany, and moved to the United States at the age of three. He attended elementary school in Shell Rock, Iowa, and spent one year of high school in Williamsport, Pennsylvania. He was a senior at Clarksville High School when he was killed in car accident in November of 1970.

Mike Heffner is from Williamsport, Pennsylvania, where he met Willie Fokkena in high school. In the early days of the World Wide Web, Mike searched for the name "Fokkena" and found Habbo Fokkena, Willie's brother, which is how Mike became involved with this project. He now lives in Muncy, Pennsylvania with his wife, Kim, and his son, Jacob, who is an athlete on both field and ice.

Clara (Fokkena) Hinman grew up in Evansdale, Iowa, and received her teaching degree from the University of Northern Iowa in 1968. She is a teacher at Clarksville Elementary School in Clarksville, Iowa, where she lives with her husband, Wayne Hinman. Clara has made half a dozen extended trips to Europe, including a year teaching elementary school in Vicenza, Italy. She once took twenty second-graders to visit a porcelain glass factory in Nove, Italy. "Once," because it's the kind of thing a person doesn't do twice.

Joelle Kasprisin is the daughter of Heidi Sandler and Steve Kasprisin. She lives in Bartlett, Illinois, and loves reading, languages, and music. Joelle has also been involved in many areas of her youth group at Living Lord Lutheran Church. She wants to study medicine when she is older, and is learning computer skills. She also wants to learn to yodel.

Katharina More is the daughter of Heidi Sandler and Angus More. She lives in Bartlett, Illinois, and is learning computer skills and sewing. She plans to have a career in fashion, but Katie also loves working with children, and is a youth group member and volunteer at Living Lord Lutheran Church. Katie is in charge of all hair and clothing decisions in her household.

Jens Pfeifer grew up in Oldenburg, Germany, and is currently studying at the School of Audio Engineering in Hamburg. Jens is a musician, a music producer, a lover of high-tech communication, and the grandson of an excellent grand-mother.

Becky Sandler moved from East Grand Forks, Minnesota to the big city of Chicago in 1971, where she later met and married Mike Sandler (father of Heidi and Phil). Becky and Mike live now in Elk Grove Village, Illinois, where Becky works in customer service, helps raise her grandchildren, Katie and Joelle, and is addicted to home-improvement-reality-television.

Heidi Sandler was born in Skokie, Illinois, but lives now in Bartlett, Illinois, where she is a technical writer and a church youth group volunteer. She studied at Northern Illinois University, earning a BA in German Language and Literature and an MA in English Linguistics. Although she has lived in Nürnberg, Germany, and has traveled to Aurich over a dozen times, she still does not drink beer or tea. Ever.

Phil Sandler lives and works in Chicago, Illinois, where he is a computer consultant. He was born in Skokie, Illinois and has studied both English and computer science. Phil is also a volleyball player and a poker enthusiast, though none of us are sure how good he actually is at either hobby.

The Stammtisch Collective is made up of Mario Ewert, Laura Fokkena, Jens Pfeifer, and Heidi Sandler. It began as a group of friends talking in an online chatroom, and ended up as a group of friends talking on a porch in small-town Iowa.

Gerda (Fecht) Taylor was born in Wiesens, Germany, and came to America as a young woman. She has lived in the Chicago area ever since, but has traveled back and forth between Germany and Illinois many times. Gerda is the parish secretary of Living Lord Lutheran Church in Bartlett, Illinois, where she is a Stephen Minister and a humanitarian. She is also Oma to her two granddaughters and their friends, and a beloved maker of pancakes.

0-595-32683-8

www.ingramcontent.com/pod-product-compliance
Lightning Source LLC
Chambersburg PA
CBHW061401280526
45784CB00001B/327